fast food
far east

QUICK AND EASY DISHES
WITH ASIAN FLAVOURS

Consultant Editor: LINDA DOESER

LORENZ BOOKS

First published in 1999 by Lorenz Books

© Anness Publishing Limited 1999

Lorenz Books is an imprint of
Anness Publishing Limited
Hermes House
88–89 Blackfriars Road
London SE1 8HA

ISBN 0 7548 0115 2

A CIP catalogue record for this book is available from the British Library.

Publisher: Joanna Lorenz
Cookery Editor: Linda Doeser
Copy Editor: Harriette Lanzer
Designer: Ian Sandom
Illustrations: Madeleine David

Front cover: Lisa Tai, Designer; William Lingwood, Photographer;
Helen Trent, Stylist; Sunil Vijayakar, Home Economist

Photographers: Karl Adamson, Edward Allwright, David Armstorng,
Steve Baxter, James Duncan, Michelle Garrett, Amanda Heywood,
Patrick McLeavey, Michael Michaels, Thomas Odulate
Stylists: Madeleine Brehaut, Michelle Garrett, Maria Kelly,
Blake Minton, Kirsty Rawlings
Food for Photography: Carla Capalbo, Kit Chan, Joanne Craig, Nicola Fowler,
Carole Handslip, Jane Hartshorn, Shehzad Husain, Wendy Lee, Lucy McKelvie,
Annie Nichols, Jane Stevenson, Steven Wheeler, Elizabeth Wolf-Cohen

Previously published as part of a larger compendium, *The Ultimate Chinese & Asian Cookbook*

Printed in Hong Kong/China

1 3 5 7 9 10 8 6 4 2

NOTES
For all recipes, quantities are given in both metric and imperial measures, and,
where appropriate, measures are also given in standard cups and spoons. Follow
one set, but not a mixture, because they are not interchangeable.

Standard spoon and cup measurements are level.
1 tsp = 5ml; 1 tbsp = 15ml; 1 cup = 250ml/8fl oz

Australian standard tablespoons are 20ml. Australian readers should use 3 tsp in
place of 1 tbsp for measuring small quantities of gelatine, cornflour, salt etc.

Medium eggs should be used unless otherwise stated.

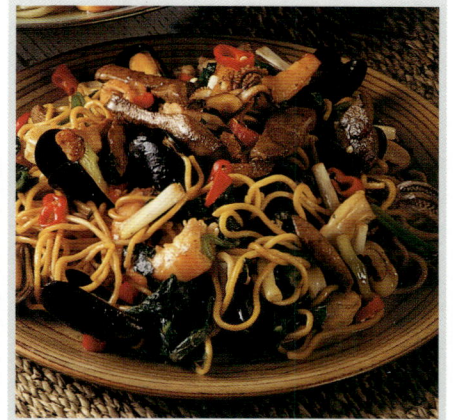

CONTENTS

Introduction 6

Soups & Appetizers *14*

Fish & Shellfish *26*

Meat & Poultry Dishes *42*

Vegetables & Vegetarian Dishes *60*

Rice & Noodle Dishes *78*

Desserts *90*

Index *96*

INTRODUCTION

Fast food was virtually invented in the Far East and stir-frying is probably the oldest rapid-cooking technique in the world. Throughout the towns and villages of China and South-east Asia, the streets and market places are lined with stalls selling fresh, fast-cooking snacks and meals, ready at a moment's notice at any time of day.

Stir-frying was invented and perfected by the Chinese and quickly spread throughout Asia – from Thailand to Japan and from India to Malaysia. The secret is to prepare all the ingredients in advance, dicing or slicing them to the same size so that they can be cooked rapidly and evenly as they are constantly tossed in hot oil in a wok. Originally designed for cooking over an open fire, the wok has a rounded base and sloping sides. This ensures that the heat spreads quickly and evenly, so that ingredients keep their colour, texture, aroma and flavour.

However, stir-frying is only half the story. Delicious dishes can be cooked just as quickly by other methods. Steaming – usually in a bamboo steamer placed over the wok – is a favourite technique and is especially well suited to delicate ingredients, such as fish and green vegetables. The wok is so versatile that it can also be used for poaching, braising and deep-frying.

All the recipes in this superb collection can be prepared in a maximum of 20 minutes and most of them take less time still. This book will convince you that fast food Far East style can be delicious, nutritious and exciting.

The Wok

The wok, a cross between a saucepan and a frying pan, is one of the world's oldest cooking utensils and developed because the Chinese made a virtue of necessity. Fuel was, and still is, scarce in China, so someone ingeniously developed a metal pan with a rounded base and sloping sides that ensured food cooked as rapidly and evenly as possible, conserving meagre supplies of wood and, co-incidentally, preserving the flavour, texture, colour and aroma of the ingredients.

Although originally made of iron, woks are now available in a variety of materials. These include cast iron, stainless steel, copper, aluminium and even ones with a non-stick lining. However, stainless steel woks have a tendency to scorch and non-stick woks cannot be heated to the very high temperatures that are really required for stir-frying. They may have one long handle or two shorter, ear-shaped handles either side. Some have a long handle one side and a short handle

opposite. Wooden handles are safer than metal. Woks are available in a range of sizes. One with a diameter of 35cm/14in is a useful size for most families. Make sure that there is plenty of room in the wok for ingredients to be scooped and tossed constantly.

Woks are available in a wide variety of materials and sizes. Some are supplied with a range of accessories and these can also be bought separately.

Some woks come with a stand, which enables them to fit more securely on modern hobs. Otherwise, a stand can be purchased separately and may be very useful. It is essential if you are using the wok for deep-frying, as an unsteady wok would be very dangerous. Stands are made of metal and may be a simple open-sided frame or a metal ring with holes punched around the side.

A wooden or metal trivet may also be included or can be bought separately. While not essential, it is useful for steaming. Bamboo steamers in a range of sizes are ideal for steaming. The steamer rests just inside the wok above the water and additional baskets can be stacked one on top of the other for cooking a number of dishes simultaneously.

A domed lid is a useful accessory, but not essential. It is helpful when you use the wok for steaming, as it allows plenty of space for the steam to circulate and the condensed water runs down the sides without dripping on the food. However, a large, snug-fitting saucepan lid is adequate.

SEASONING AND CLEANING THE WOK

Apart from those with a non-stick lining, new woks must be seasoned before use. First, scrub off the manufacturer's protective coating of oil with cream cleanser and plenty of hot water. Rinse and thoroughly dry the wok. Place it over a low heat and add about 30ml/2 tbsp vegetable oil, rubbing the oil over the entire inside surface with a thick pad of kitchen paper. Be careful not to burn your fingers. Gently heat the wok for about 10-15 minutes, then wipe off the oil with more kitchen paper, which will become black. Repeat this process of coating, heating and wiping until the kitchen paper remains clean. Make sure the wok is cool enough to handle when you are doing this. When the paper remains clean, the wok is seasoned and ready for use.

Once seasoned, the wok should not be scrubbed or washed in detergent again. Simply rinse it thoroughly in hot water and dry well before storing. If not used frequently, the wok may turn rusty. In that case, scour off all traces of rust and season the wok again.

Keep heating the wok with a layer of oil and wiping it with kitchen paper until no traces of black remain on the paper pad.

STIR-FRYING

You can use a heavy-based frying pan rather than a wok, but it is harder to keep the ingredients moving constantly.

1 Place the wok over a high heat and preheat until very hot. Add the oil and swirl it so that it coats the base and halfway up the side of the wok. Heat until it is very hot, but not smoking, so that when the ingredients are added, they start to cook immediately.

2 Add the ingredients in the order specified in the recipe – usually, aromatics, such as ginger, garlic and spring onions first, followed shortly afterwards by the ingredients that require the longest cooking time, such as meat, fish or denser vegetables, and finally, the really quick-cooking ingredients, sauces and herbs. Sometimes, meat is almost completely cooked, then removed from the wok while other ingredients are stir-fried, and then returned to the wok towards the end to finish cooking and heat through. Keep the ingredients moving all the time, scooping them from the centre and tossing them to the sides.

Preparation Techniques

SPRING ONIONS
In Far Eastern cooking, the appearance of food is as important as its taste.

1 Trim off the roots and remove any wilted ends or leaves using a sharp knife or Chinese cleaver.

2 To cut into rings, line up the spring onions and cut straight across.

3 To slice diagonally, hold the knife at an angle of about 60 degrees and slice thickly to create even-sized chunks with a large surface area.

4 To shred, cut the spring onions into 5cm/2in lengths, then slice each piece in half lengthways. Finally, shred each piece.

5 To make tassels to use as a garnish, cut the white part only into 6cm/2½in lengths. Shred one end of each piece, keeping the other end intact. Place in iced water for about 30 minutes, until the shreds curl.

FRESH ROOT GINGER
Always use a very sharp knife to ensure that the pieces are an even size.

1 Trim the ginger, removing any knobbly bits. Using a swivel vegetable peeler or a small, sharp knife, peel off the skin.

2 Hold the ginger firmly with one hand and cut diagonally into evenly thin slices.

3 To shred, stack several slices of ginger on top of each other and cut carefully into thin shreds. To chop, gather the shreds together and cut across them to make very fine pieces, then continue to chop.

CARROTS
These techniques can be used for other firm vegetables, such as courgettes.

1 Peel using a swivel vegetable peeler and trim off the ends.

2 To cut rounds, hold the carrot firmly with one hand and cut straight across into thin slices.

3 To slice diagonally, hold the knife blade at an angle of about 60 degrees and cut the carrot into thin slices with the maximum surface area.

4 To cut matchsticks, first thinly slice the carrot diagonally, as described in Step 3. Stack two or three slices and then cut them into matchsticks. Repeat with the remaining slices.

5 To make rolling cuts, hold one end of the trimmed and peeled carrot and cut off the other end diagonally into a fairly thick slice. Roll the carrot through 180 degrees and cut another diagonal slice to make a triangular wedge. Continue to roll and slice the remaining carrot in the same way.

ONIONS

Whether finely or roughly chopped, the method is the same.

1 Cut off the stalk end of the onion. Cut the onion in half through the root, leaving the root intact. Remove the skin and place the halved onion, cut side down, on a chopping board. Make lengthways vertical cuts, taking care not to cut right through to the root.

2 Make two or three horizontal cuts from the stalk end through up to the root.

3 Cut the onion across from the stalk end to the root, and it will fall away in small dice.

DRIED MUSHROOMS AND FUNGI

Wood ears and cloud ears are prepared in the same way as dried mushrooms.

1 Soak the dried mushrooms or fungi in a bowl of hot water for about 30 minutes, or until softened. Drain, rinse thoroughly and drain again.

2 Remove and discard the stalks from the soaked mushrooms and use the caps whole, sliced or chopped.

3 Cut the soaked wood ears or cloud ears into small pieces, discarding the tough base.

LEMON GRASS

You can use the whole stem for flavouring or finely chop the bulb.

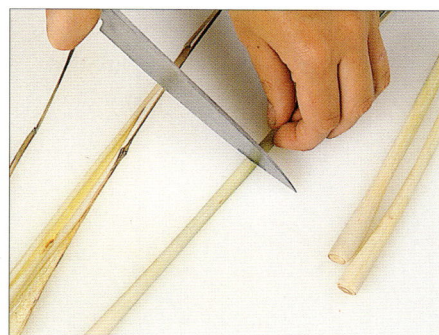

1 Trim the end of the stem and cut off the tops, leaving about 10cm/4in.

2 Split the lemon grass in half and chop finely or, if the bulb is particularly fresh, slice thinly.

CHINESE LEAVES

Whether you are using the long, pointed or shorter, barrel-shaped variety, prepare them in the same way.

1 Stack several leaves together and cut into slices or shred finely as needed.

BEANSPROUTS

Fresh beansprouts are widely available from supermarkets all year round.

1 Carefully pick over the beansprouts, discarding any that are discoloured, broken or wilted.

2 Rinse the beansprouts under cold running water and drain well. Some people like to blanch them briefly first in lightly salted boiling water.

GARLIC

A garlic press is not essential for crushing garlic. This technique produces wonderful, juicy results.

1 Break off a clove of garlic, place the flat side of a large knife on top and strike it firmly with your other fist. Remove all the papery outer skin, then finely chop the clove.

2 Sprinkle the chopped garlic with a little table salt and, using the flat side of a large knife blade, gently work the salt into the garlic until the clove softens and releases its juices.

CHILLIES

If you like very spicy flavours, use the seeds in your cooking, too.

1 Always protect your hands, as chillies can irritate the skin, and never rub your eyes after handling chillies. Trim off the stalk.

2 Halve the chilli lengthways, then remove and discard the seeds using the point of a knife.

3 Slice and finely chop the flesh. Wash the knife and board thoroughly in hot soapy water and then wash your hands well, even if you have worn protective gloves.

4 Alternatively, hold the chilli in position on the chopping board with a table fork and trim, cut and seed it using a small, sharp kitchen knife to avoid touching it with your hands.

HERBS

Chop fresh herbs just before you use them to preserve their flavour.

1 Remove the leaves. Choose a large sharp knife or Chinese cleaver, as a blunt knife will bruise rather than chop the herbs.

2 Chop the herbs as finely or coarsely as required by holding the tip of the blade on the board with the fingers of one hand and rocking the handle up and down in a see-saw motion.

3 A quick alternative for preparing herbs which do not have coarse stems is simply to hold a small bunch of them in one hand and snip the leaves with kitchen scissors.

DRIED SHRIMP AND SHRIMP PASTE

Salted and dried tiny shrimp are used as a flavouring in many Thai dishes. Dried shrimp paste is known as terasi.

1 Soak the shrimps in warm water until soft, then either process in a food processor or pound in a mortar with a pestle.

MEAT

Meat for stir-frying and sometimes steaming is cut into thin slices, matchstick strips or cubes.

1 Beef is always cut across the grain, otherwise it would become tough. Pork, lamb or chicken can be cut either along or across the grain.

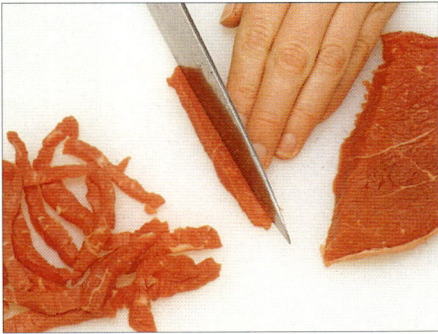

2 Placing the meat in the freezer for about 30 minutes beforehand makes it easier to cut wafer-thin slices.

MUSSELS

To ensure that any shellfish is really fresh, it is best bought still alive.

1 Thoroughly scrub the shells with a stiff brush and rinse well to remove all traces of sand and grit. This is usually best done under cold running water.

2 Pull off the "beards" with the help of a small, sharp knife. Rinse thoroughly again. Discard any mussels with damaged shells and any that do not shut immediately when sharply tapped with the back of a knife.

PRAWNS

While not harmful, the black vein may spoil the flavour if not removed.

1 Holding the prawn firmly in one hand, pull off the legs with the fingers of the other hand.

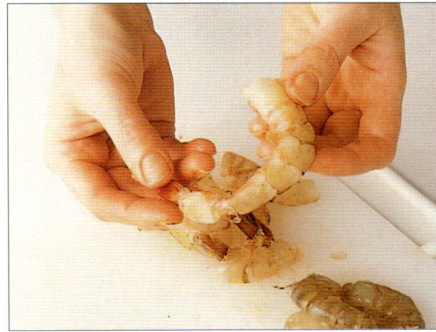

2 Peel the shell away from the body. When you reach the tail, hold the body and firmly pull away the tail; the shell will come off with it.

3 Make a shallow cut down the centre of the curved back of the prawn with a sharp knife or Chinese cleaver. Using the tip, pull out and discard the black vein that runs along the length of the body.

SQUID

Large or small, squid are easy to prepare once you know how.

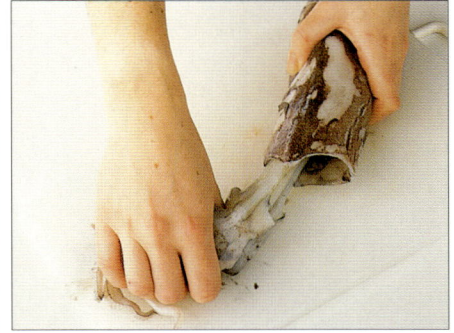

1 Gently pull away the head and tentacles. Discard the head, then trim and reserve the tentacles.

2 Remove the transparent "quill" from inside the body of the squid, then peel off the purple skin. Rub a little salt into the squid and wash well.

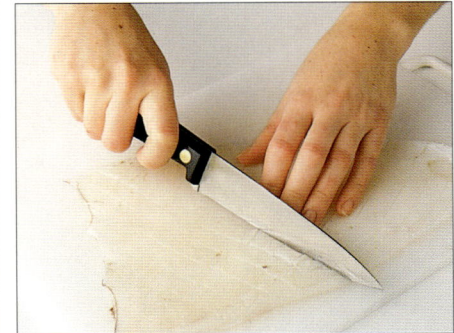

3 You can slice the body of the squid into rings or slit it open lengthways, score criss-cross patterns on the inside and cut it into pieces. The tentacles and the fins, once skinned, are also edible.

SOUPS & APPETIZERS

~

Pork and Noodle Broth with Prawns

This delicately flavoured Vietnamese soup is very quick and easy to make, but tastes really special.

INGREDIENTS

Serves 4–6
350g/12oz pork chops or fillet
225g/8oz raw prawn tails or
  cooked prawns
150g/5oz thin egg noodles
15ml/1 tbsp vegetable oil
10ml/2 tsp sesame oil
4 shallots or 1 medium onion, sliced
15ml/1 tbsp finely sliced fresh
  root ginger
1 garlic clove, crushed
5ml/1 tsp sugar
1.5 litres/2½ pints/6¼ cups
  chicken stock
2 kaffir lime leaves
45ml/3 tbsp fish sauce
juice of ½ lime
4 sprigs fresh coriander and 2 spring
  onions, green parts only, chopped,
  to garnish

1 If you are using pork chops, trim away any fat. Place the meat in the freezer for 30 minutes to firm, but not freeze, it. Slice the pork thinly and set aside. Peel and devein the prawns, if using raw prawn tails.

2 Bring a large saucepan of salted water to the boil and simmer the noodles according to the instructions on the packet. Drain and refresh under cold running water. Set aside.

3 Heat the vegetable and sesame oils in a preheated wok, add the shallots or onion and stir-fry for 3–4 minutes, until evenly browned. Remove from the wok and set aside.

4 Add the ginger, garlic, sugar and chicken stock to the wok and bring to a simmer. Add the lime leaves, fish sauce and lime juice. Add the pork, then simmer for 15 minutes. Add the prawns and noodles and simmer for 3–4 minutes to heat through. Serve in shallow bowls, garnished with coriander sprigs, the green parts of the spring onion and the browned shallots or onion.

Spinach and Tofu Soup

If fresh young spinach leaves are not available, watercress or lettuce can be used instead. Sorrel leaves may also be used as a substitute, but they have a stronger and slightly more bitter flavour than spinach.

INGREDIENTS

Serves 4

1 packet tofu
115g/4oz spinach leaves
750ml/1¼ pints/3 cups stock
15ml/1 tbsp light soy sauce
salt and ground black pepper

1 Cut the tofu into 12 small pieces, each about 5mm/¼in thick. Wash the spinach leaves and cut them into small pieces.

2 Bring the stock to a rolling boil in a wok. Add the tofu and soy sauce, bring back to the boil and simmer for about 2 minutes.

3 Add the spinach and simmer for a further minute. Skim the surface to make it clear, then adjust the seasoning and serve immediately.

COOK'S TIP

Fresh tofu is sold in cakes about 7.5cm/3in square in Chinese food stores. Do not confuse it with fermented tofu, which is much stronger-tasting, quite salty and usually used as a condiment.

Sliced Fish and Coriander Soup

It is not necessary to remove the skin from the fish, as it helps to keep the flesh together when poached in the wok.

INGREDIENTS

Serves 4

225g/8oz white fish fillets, such as
  lemon sole or plaice
15ml/1 tbsp egg white
10ml/2 tsp cornflour paste
750ml/1¼ pints/3 cups stock
15ml/1 tbsp light soy sauce
about 50g/2oz fresh coriander
  leaves, chopped
salt and ground black pepper

1 Cut the fish into slices, each about the size of a matchbox. Mix with the egg white and cornflour paste.

2 Bring the stock to a rolling boil in a wok and poach the fish slices for about 1 minute.

3 Add the soy sauce and coriander leaves, adjust the seasoning and serve immediately.

Chicken and Buckwheat Noodle Soup

Buckwheat or soba noodles are widely enjoyed in Japan. The simplest way of serving them is in hot seasoned broth. Almost any topping can be added and the variations are endless.

INGREDIENTS

Serves 4

225g/8oz skinless, boneless
  chicken breasts
120ml/4fl oz/½ cup soy sauce
15ml/1 tbsp saké
1 litre/1¾ pints/4 cups chicken stock
2 pieces young leek, cut into
  2.5cm/1in pieces
175g/6oz spinach leaves
300g/11oz buckwheat or
  soba noodles
sesame seeds, toasted, to garnish

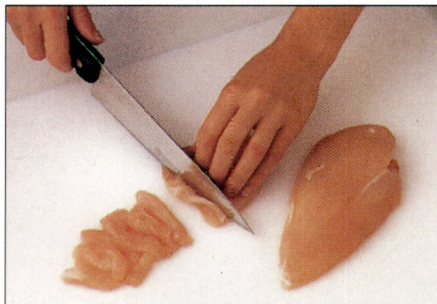

1 Slice the chicken diagonally into bite-size pieces. Combine the soy sauce and saké in a saucepan. Bring to a simmer. Add the chicken and cook gently for about 3 minutes until it is tender. Keep hot.

2 Bring the stock to the boil in a saucepan. Add the leek and simmer for 3 minutes, then add the spinach. Remove from the heat but keep warm.

3 Cook the noodles in a large saucepan of boiling water until just tender, following the manufacturer's directions on the packet.

4 Drain the noodles and divide among individual serving bowls. Ladle the hot soup into the bowls, then add a portion of chicken to each. Serve at once, sprinkled with sesame seeds.

COOK'S TIP

Home-made chicken stock makes the world of difference to noodle soup. Make a big batch of stock, use as much as you need and freeze the rest until required. Put about 1.5kg/3–3½lb meaty chicken bones into a large saucepan, add 3 litres/5 pints/ 12½ cups water and slowly bring to the boil, skimming off any foam that rises to the top. Add 2 slices fresh root ginger, 2 garlic cloves, 2 celery sticks, 4 spring onions, a handful of coriander stalks and about 10 peppercorns, crushed, then reduce the heat and simmer the stock for 2–2½ hours. Remove from the heat and leave to cool, uncovered and undisturbed. Strain the stock into a clean bowl, leaving the last dregs behind as they tend to cloud the soup. Use as required, removing any fat that congeals on top.

Miso Breakfast Soup

Miso is a fermented bean paste that adds richness and flavour to many of Japan's favourite soups. It is available in health food stores. This unusual soup provides a nourishing start to the day.

INGREDIENTS

Serves 4

3 shiitake mushrooms, fresh or dried
1.2 litres/2 pints/5 cups vegetable stock
60ml/4 tbsp miso paste
115g/4oz tofu, cut into large dice
1 spring onion, green part only, sliced, to garnish

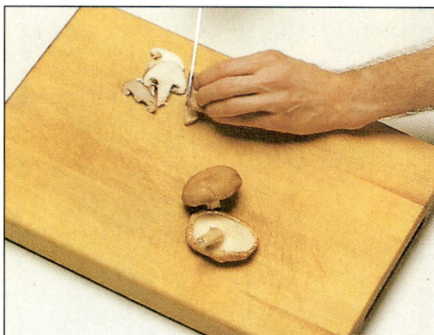

1 If using dried mushrooms, soak them in hot water for 3–4 minutes, then drain. Slice the mushrooms thinly and set aside.

2 Bring the stock to the boil in a large saucepan. Stir in the miso paste and mushrooms, lower the heat and simmer for 5 minutes.

3 Ladle the broth into 4 soup bowls and divide the tofu between them. Sprinkle over the spring onion and serve immediately.

Quick-fried Prawns with Hot Spices

These spicy prawns are stir-fried in moments to make a wonderful starter. Don't forget that you will need to provide your guests with finger bowls.

INGREDIENTS

Serves 4

450g/1lb large raw prawns
2.5cm/1in fresh root ginger, grated
2 garlic cloves, crushed
5ml/1 tsp hot chilli powder
5ml/1 tsp ground turmeric
10ml/2 tsp black mustard seeds
seeds from 4 green cardamom
   pods, crushed
50g/2oz/4 tbsp ghee or butter
120ml/4fl oz/½ cup coconut milk
salt and ground black pepper
30–45ml/2–3 tbsp chopped fresh
   coriander, to garnish
naan bread, to serve

1 Peel the prawns carefully, leaving the tails attached.

2 Using a small sharp knife, make a slit along the back of each prawn and remove the dark vein. Rinse under cold running water, drain and pat dry.

3 Put the ginger, garlic, chilli powder, turmeric, mustard seeds and cardamom seeds in a bowl. Add the prawns and toss to coat completely with spice mixture.

4 Heat a wok until hot. Add the ghee or butter and swirl it around until foaming.

5 Add the marinated prawns and stir-fry for 1–1½ minutes until they are just turning pink.

6 Stir in the coconut milk and simmer for 3–4 minutes until the prawns are just cooked through. Season to taste with salt and pepper. Sprinkle over the coriander and serve at once with naan bread.

Crab and Tofu Dumplings

These little crab and ginger-flavoured dumplings are usually served as a delicious side dish as part of a Japanese meal.

INGREDIENTS

Serves 4–6

115g/4oz frozen white crab meat, thawed
115g/4oz tofu
1 egg yolk
30ml/2 tbsp rice flour or wheat flour
30ml/2 tbsp finely chopped spring onion, green part only
2cm/¾in fresh root ginger, grated
10ml/2 tsp light soy sauce
salt
vegetable oil, for deep-frying
50g/2oz mooli, very finely grated, to serve

For the dipping sauce

120ml/4fl oz vegetable stock
15ml/1 tbsp sugar
45ml/3 tbsp dark soy sauce

1 Squeeze as much moisture out of the crab meat as you can. Press the tofu through a fine strainer with the back of a tablespoon. Combine the tofu and crab meat in a bowl.

2 Add the egg yolk, rice or wheat flour, spring onion, ginger and soy sauce and season to taste with salt. Mix thoroughly to form a light paste.

3 To make the dipping sauce, combine the stock, sugar and soy sauce in a serving bowl.

4 Line a tray with kitchen paper. Heat the vegetable oil in a wok or frying pan to 190°C/375°F. Meanwhile, shape the crab and tofu mixture into thumb-sized pieces. Fry in batches of three at a time for 1–2 minutes. Drain on the kitchen paper and serve with the sauce and mooli.

Sweet Potato and Pumpkin Prawn Cakes

Serve these fried cakes warm with a fish sauce.

INGREDIENTS

Serves 4–6

200g/7oz strong white bread flour
2.5ml/½ tsp salt
2.5ml/½ tsp dried yeast
175ml/6fl oz/¾ cup hand-hot water
1 egg, beaten
200g/7oz fresh prawn tails, peeled and
  roughly chopped
150g/5oz sweet potato, peeled
  and grated
225g/8oz pumpkin, peeled, seeded
  and grated
2 spring onions, chopped
50g/2oz water chestnuts, sliced
  and chopped
2.5ml/½ tsp chilli sauce
1 clove garlic, crushed
juice of ½ lime
30–45ml/2–3 tbsp vegetable oil
spring onions, to garnish

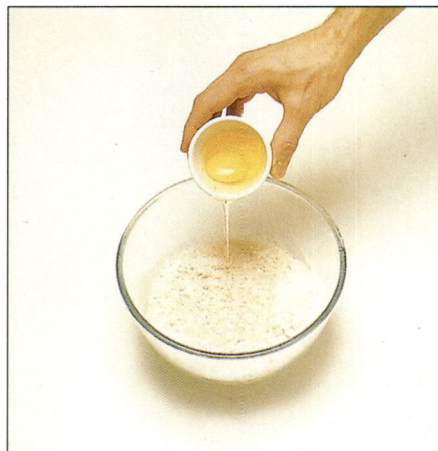

1 Sift the flour and salt into a mixing bowl and make a well in the centre. Dissolve the yeast in the water, then pour into the well. Pour in the egg and leave for a few minutes until bubbles appear. Mix to a batter.

2 Place the peeled prawns in a saucepan and cover with water. Bring to the boil and simmer for 10–12 minutes. Drain, refresh in cold water and drain again. Roughly chop and set the prawns aside.

3 Add the sweet potato and pumpkin to the batter, then add the spring onions, water chestnuts, chilli sauce, garlic, lime juice and prawns. Heat a little oil in a wok or frying pan. Spoon in the batter in small heaps and fry until golden. Drain and serve, garnished with spring onions.

Fish Cakes with Cucumber Relish

These wonderful small fish cakes are a very familiar and popular appetizer. They are usually accompanied with Thai beer.

INGREDIENTS

Makes about 12

300g/11oz white fish fillet, such as cod, cut into chunks
30ml/2 tbsp red curry paste
1 egg
30ml/2 tbsp fish sauce
5ml/1 tsp granulated sugar
30ml/2 tbsp cornflour
3 kaffir lime leaves, shredded
15ml/1 tbsp chopped coriander
50g/2oz green beans, finely sliced
oil for frying
Chinese mustard cress, to garnish

For the cucumber relish

60ml/4 tbsp Thai coconut or rice vinegar
60ml/4 tbsp water
50g/2oz sugar
1 head pickled garlic
1 cucumber, quartered and sliced
4 shallots, finely sliced
15ml/1 tbsp finely chopped root ginger

1 To make the cucumber relish, bring the vinegar, water and sugar to the boil. Stir until the sugar dissolves, then remove from the heat and cool.

2 Combine the rest of the relish ingredients together in a bowl and pour over the vinegar mixture.

3 Combine the fish, curry paste and egg in a food processor and process well. Transfer the mixture to a bowl, add the rest of the ingredients, except for the oil and garnish, and mix well.

4 Mould and shape the mixture into cakes about 5cm/2in in diameter and 5mm/¼in thick.

5 Heat the oil in a wok or deep-fat fryer. Fry the fish cakes, a few at a time, for about 4–5 minutes or until golden brown. Remove and drain on kitchen paper. Garnish with Chinese mustard cress and serve with the cucumber relish.

Spicy Meat Patties with Coconut

Spicy meat patties, known as *Rempah*, with a hint of coconut, often feature as one of the delicious accompaniments in an Indonesian-style buffet.

INGREDIENTS

Makes 22

115g/4oz freshly grated coconut, or desiccated coconut, soaked in 60–90ml/4–6 tbsp boiling water
350g/12oz finely minced beef
2.5ml/½ tsp each coriander and cumin seeds, dry-fried
1 garlic clove, crushed
a little beaten egg
15–30ml/1–2 tbsp plain flour
groundnut oil for frying
salt
thin lemon or lime wedges, to serve

1 Mix the moistened coconut with the minced beef.

2 Grind the dry-fried coriander and cumin seeds with a pestle and mortar. Add the ground spices to the meat and coconut mixture together with the garlic, salt to taste, and sufficient beaten egg to bind.

3 Divide the meat into evenly sized portions, the size of a walnut, and form into patty shapes.

4 Dust with flour. Heat the oil and then fry the patties for 4–5 minutes until both sides are golden brown and cooked through. Serve with lemon or lime wedges, to squeeze over.

Sweetcorn Fritters

There is no doubt that freshly cooked sweetcorn is best for this recipe, called *Perkedel Jagung*. Do not add salt to the water, because this toughens the outer husk.

INGREDIENTS

Makes 20

2 fresh corn on the cob, or 350g/12oz can sweetcorn kernels
2 macadamia nuts or 4 almonds
1 garlic clove
1 onion, quartered
1cm/½in fresh *lengkuas*, peeled and sliced
5ml/1 tsp ground coriander
30–45ml/2–3 tbsp oil
3 eggs, beaten
30ml/2 tbsp desiccated coconut
2 spring onions, finely shredded
a few celery leaves, finely shredded (optional)
salt

1 Cook the corn on the cob in boiling water for 7–8 minutes. Drain, cool slightly and, using a sharp knife, strip the kernels from the cob. If using canned sweetcorn, drain well.

2 Grind the nuts, garlic, onion, *lengkuas* and coriander to a fine paste in a food processor or pestle and mortar. Heat a little oil and fry the paste until it gives off a spicy aroma.

3 Add the fried spices to the beaten eggs with the coconut, spring onions and celery leaves, if using. Add salt to taste with the corn kernels.

4 Heat the remaining oil in a shallow frying pan. Drop large spoonfuls of batter into the pan and cook for 2–3 minutes until golden. Flip the fritters over with a fish slice and cook until golden brown and crispy. Only cook three or four fritters at a time.

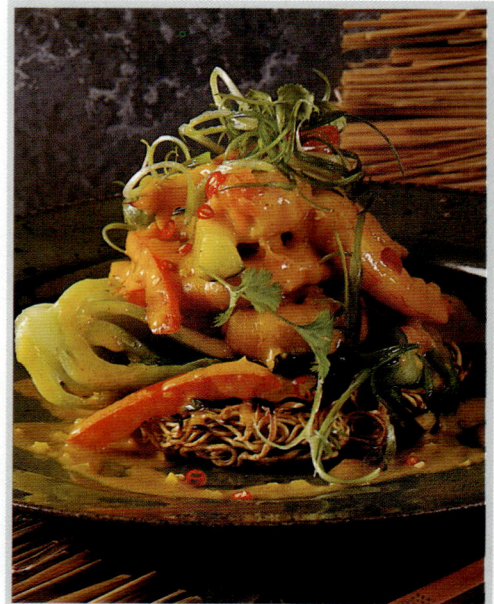

FISH & SEAFOOD

~

Chinese-spiced Fish Fillets

INGREDIENTS

Serves 4

65g/2½oz/generous ½ cup plain flour
5ml/1 tsp Chinese five-spice powder
8 skinless fillets of fish, such as plaice or
  lemon sole, about 800g/1¾lb in total
1 egg, lightly beaten
40–50g/1½–2oz/scant 1 cup fine
  fresh breadcrumbs
groundnut oil, for frying
25g/1oz/2 tbsp butter
4 spring onions, cut diagonally into
  thin slices
350g/12oz tomatoes, seeded and diced
30ml/2 tbsp soy sauce
salt and ground black pepper
red pepper strips and chives, to garnish

1 Sift the flour together with the Chinese five-spice powder and salt and pepper to taste on to a plate. Dip the fish fillets first in the seasoned flour, then in the beaten egg and finally in breadcrumbs.

2 Pour oil into a large frying pan to a depth of 1cm/½ in. Heat until it is very hot and starting to sizzle. Add the coated fillets, a few at a time, and fry for 2–3 minutes on each side, depending on their thickness, until just cooked and golden brown. Do not crowd the pan, or the temperature of the oil will drop and the fish will absorb too much of it.

3 Drain the fillets on kitchen paper, then transfer to serving plates and keep warm. Pour off all the oil from the frying pan and wipe it out with kitchen paper.

4 Cook the spring onions and tomatoes in the butter for 1 minute, then add the soy sauce.

5 Spoon the tomato mixture over the fish, garnish with red pepper strips and chives and serve.

Salmon Teriyaki

Marinating the salmon makes it so wonderfully tender, it just melts in the mouth, and the crunchy condiment provides an excellent foil.

INGREDIENTS
Serves 4
675g/1½lb salmon fillet
30ml/2 tbsp sunflower oil
watercress, to garnish

For the teriyaki sauce
5ml/1 tsp caster sugar
5ml/1 tsp dry white wine
5ml/1 tsp sake, rice wine or
 dry sherry
30ml/2 tbsp dark soy sauce

For the condiment
5cm/2in fresh root ginger, grated
pink food colouring (optional)
50g/2oz mooli, grated

1 For the teriyaki sauce, mix together the sugar, white wine, sake or rice wine or dry sherry and soy sauce, stirring until the sugar dissolves.

2 Remove the skin from the salmon using a very sharp filleting knife.

3 Cut the fillet into strips, then place in a non-metallic dish. Pour over the teriyaki sauce and set aside to marinate for 10–15 minutes.

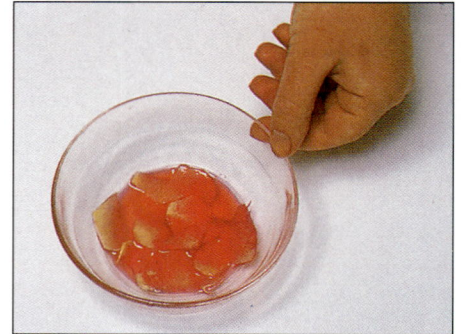

4 To make the condiment, place the ginger in a bowl and add a little pink food colouring if you wish. Stir in the mooli.

5 Lift the salmon from the teriyaki sauce and drain.

6 Heat the oil in a preheated wok. Add the salmon in batches and stir-fry for 3–4 minutes, until it is cooked. Transfer to serving plates, garnish with the watercress and serve with the mooli and ginger condiment.

Vinegar Fish

Fish cooked in a spicy mixture that includes chillies, ginger and vinegar is an Indonesian speciality. It is a method that lends itself particularly well to strong-flavoured, oily fish, such as the mackerel used here.

INGREDIENTS

Serves 2–3

2–3 mackerel, filleted
2-3 red chillies, seeded
4 macadamia nuts or 8 almonds
1 red onion, quartered
2 garlic cloves, crushed
1cm/½in piece root ginger, peeled
  and sliced
5ml/1 tsp ground turmeric
45ml/3 tbsp coconut or vegetable oil
45ml/3 tbsp wine vinegar
150ml/¼ pint/⅔ cup water
salt
deep-fried onions and finely chopped
  chilli, to garnish
boiled or coconut rice, to
  serve (optional)

1 Rinse the mackerel fillets in cold water and dry well on kitchen paper. Set aside.

COOK'S TIP

To make coconut rice, put 400g/14oz washed long grain rice in a heavy saucepan with 2.5ml/½ tsp salt, a 5cm/2in piece of lemon grass and 25g/1oz creamed coconut. Add 750ml/1¼ pints/3 cups boiling water and stir once to prevent the grains sticking together. Simmer over a medium heat for 10–12 minutes. Remove the pan from the heat, cover and set aside for 5 minutes. Fluff the rice with a fork or chopsticks before serving.

---

2 Put the chillies, macadamia nuts or almonds, onion, garlic, ginger, turmeric and 15ml/1 tbsp of the oil in a food processor and process to form a paste. Alternatively, pound them together in a mortar with a pestle to form a paste. Heat the remaining oil in a wok. When it is hot, add the paste and cook for 1–2 minutes without browning. Stir in the vinegar and water and season with salt to taste. Bring to the boil, then lower the heat.

3 Add the mackerel fillets to the sauce and simmer for 6–8 minutes or until the fish is tender and cooked.

4 Transfer the fish to a warm serving dish. Bring the sauce to a boil and cook for 1 minute or until it has reduced slightly. Pour the sauce over the fish, garnish with the deep-fried onions and chopped chilli and serve with rice, if liked.

Fish Balls with Chinese Greens

These tasty fish balls are steamed over a wok with a selection of green vegetables – pak choi is available from oriental stores.

INGREDIENTS

Serves 4

For the fish balls
450g/1lb white fish fillets, skinned, boned and cubed
3 spring onions, chopped
1 back bacon rasher, rinded and chopped
15ml/1 tbsp Chinese rice wine
30ml/2 tbsp light soy sauce
1 egg white

For the vegetables
1 small head pak choi
5ml/1 tsp cornflour
15ml/1 tbsp light soy sauce
150ml/$^1/_4$ pint/$^2/_3$ cup cup fish stock
30ml/2 tbsp groundnut oil
2 garlic cloves, sliced
2.5cm/1in fresh root ginger, cut into thin shreds
75g/3oz green beans
175g/6oz mangetouts
3 spring onions, sliced diagonally into 5–7.5cm/2–3in lengths
salt and ground black pepper

1 Put the fish, spring onions, bacon, rice wine, soy sauce and egg white in a food processor and process until smooth. With wetted hands, form the mixture into about 24 small balls.

2 Steam the fish balls in batches in a lightly greased bamboo steamer in a wok for 5–10 minutes until cooked through and firm. Remove from the steamer and keep warm.

3 Meanwhile trim the pak choi, removing any discoloured leaves or damaged stems, then tear into manageable pieces.

4 Blend together the cornflour, soy sauce and stock in a small bowl and set aside.

5 Heat a wok until hot, add the oil and swirl it around. Add the garlic and ginger and stir-fry for 2–3 minutes. Add the beans and stir-fry for 2–3 minutes, then add the mangetouts, spring onions and pak choi. Stir-fry for 2–3 minutes.

6 Add the sauce to the wok and cook, stirring, until it has thickened and the vegetables are tender but crisp. Taste and adjust the seasoning, if necessary. Serve with the fish balls.

COOK'S TIP

You can replace the mangetouts and green beans with broccoli florets. Blanch them before stir-frying.

Spicy Fish

If you make *Ikan Kecap* a day ahead, put it straight on to a serving dish after cooking and then pour over the sauce, cover and chill until required.

INGREDIENTS

Serves 3–4
450g/1lb fish fillets, such as mackerel, cod or haddock
30ml/2 tbsp plain flour
groundnut oil for frying
1 onion, roughly chopped
1 small garlic clove, crushed
4cm/1½in fresh root ginger, peeled and grated
1–2 fresh red chillies, seeded and sliced
1cm/½in cube *terasi,* prepared
60ml/4 tbsp water
juice of ½ lemon
15ml/1 tbsp brown sugar
30ml/2 tbsp dark soy sauce
salt
roughly torn lettuce leaves, to serve

1 Rinse the fish fillets under cold water and dry well on absorbent kitchen paper. Cut into serving portions and remove any bones.

2 Season the flour with salt and use it to dust the fish. Heat the oil in a frying pan and fry the fish on both sides for 3–4 minutes, or until cooked. Lift on to a plate and set aside.

3 Rinse out and dry the pan. Heat a little more oil and fry the onion, garlic, ginger and chillies just to bring out the flavour. Do not brown.

4 Blend the *terasi* with a little water, to make a paste. Add it to the onion mixture, with a little extra water if necessary. Cook for 2 minutes and then stir in the lemon juice, brown sugar and soy sauce.

5 Pour over the fish and serve, hot or cold, with roughly torn lettuce.

COOK'S TIP

For a buffet dish cut the fish into bite-size pieces or serving portions.

Squid from Madura

This squid dish, *Cumi Cumi Madura,* is popular in Indonesia. It is quite usual to be invited into the restaurant kitchen and given a warm welcome.

INGREDIENTS

Serves 2–3
450g/1lb cleaned and drained squid, body cut in strips, tentacles left whole
3 garlic cloves
1.5ml/¼ tsp ground nutmeg
1 bunch of spring onions
60ml/4 tbsp sunflower oil
250ml/8fl oz/1 cup water
15ml/1 tbsp dark soy sauce
salt and freshly ground black pepper
1 lime, cut in wedges (optional)
boiled rice, to serve

1 Squeeze out the little central "bone" from each tentacle. Heat a wok, toss in all the squid and stir-fry for 1 minute. Remove the squid.

2 Crush the garlic with the nutmeg and some salt and pepper. Trim the roots from the spring onions, cut the white part into small pieces, slice the green part and then set aside.

3 Heat the wok, add the oil and fry the white part of the spring onions. Stir in the garlic paste and the squid.

4 Rinse out the garlic paste container with the water and soy sauce and add to the pan. Half-cover and simmer for 4–5 minutes. Add the spring onion tops, toss lightly and serve at once, with lime, if using, and rice.

Sweet-and-sour Fish

When fish is cooked in this way the skin becomes crispy on the outside, while the flesh remains moist and juicy inside. The sweet and sour sauce, with its colourful cherry tomatoes, complements the fish beautifully.

INGREDIENTS

Serves 4–6

1 large or 2 medium-size fish such as
  snapper or mullet, heads removed
20ml/4 tsp cornflour
120ml/4fl oz/½ cup vegetable oil
15ml/1 tbsp chopped garlic
15ml/1 tbsp chopped root ginger
30ml/2 tbsp chopped shallots
225g/8oz cherry tomatoes
30ml/2 tbsp red wine vinegar
30ml/2 tbsp granulated sugar
30ml/2 tbsp tomato ketchup
15ml/1 tbsp fish sauce
45ml/3 tbsp water
salt and freshly ground black pepper
coriander leaves, to garnish
shredded spring onions, to garnish

1 Thoroughly rinse and clean the fish. Score the skin diagonally on both sides of the fish.

2 Coat the fish lightly on both sides with 15ml/1 tbsp cornflour. Shake off any excess.

3 Heat the oil in a wok or large frying pan and slide the fish into the wok. Reduce the heat to medium and fry the fish until crisp and brown, about 6–7 minutes on both sides.

4 Remove the fish with a fish slice and place on a large platter.

5 Pour off all but 30ml/2 tbsp of the oil and add the garlic, ginger and shallots. Fry until golden.

6 Add the cherry tomatoes and cook until they burst open. Stir in the vinegar, sugar, tomato ketchup and fish sauce. Simmer gently for 1–2 minutes and adjust the seasoning.

7 Blend the remaining 5ml/1 tsp cornflour with the water. Stir into the sauce and heat until it thickens. Pour the sauce over the fish and garnish with coriander leaves and shredded spring onions.

Stir-fried Five-spice Squid

Squid is perfect for stir-frying as it should be cooked quickly. The spicy sauce makes the ideal accompaniment.

INGREDIENTS

Serves 6

450g/1lb small squid, cleaned
45ml/3 tbsp oil
2.5cm/1 in fresh root ginger, grated
1 garlic clove, crushed
8 spring onions, cut diagonally into
   2.5cm/1in lengths
1 red pepper, seeded and cut into strips
1 fresh green chilli, seeded and thinly
   sliced
6 mushrooms, sliced
5ml/1 tsp Chinese five-spice powder
30ml/2 tbsp black bean sauce
30ml/2 tbsp soy sauce
5ml/1 tsp sugar
15ml/1 tbsp Chinese rice wine or
   dry sherry

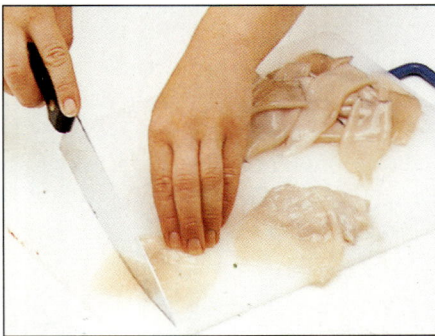

1 Rinse the squid and pull away the outer skin. Dry on kitchen paper. Slit the squid open and score the inside into diamonds with a sharp knife. Cut the squid into strips.

2 Heat the oil in a preheated wok. Stir-fry the squid quickly. Remove the squid strips from the wok with a slotted spoon and set aside. Add the ginger, garlic, spring onions, red pepper, chilli and mushrooms to the oil remaining in the wok and stir-fry for 2 minutes.

3 Return the squid to the wok and stir in the five-spice powder. Stir in the black bean sauce, soy sauce, sugar and rice wine or dry sherry. Bring to the boil and cook, stirring, for 1 minute. Serve immediately.

Lemon Grass Prawns on Crisp Noodle Cake

INGREDIENTS

Serves 4

300g/11oz thin egg noodles
60ml/4 tbsp vegetable oil
500g/1¼lb medium raw king prawns,
  peeled and deveined
2.5ml/½ tsp ground coriander
15ml/1 tbsp ground turmeric
2 garlic cloves, finely chopped
2 slices fresh root ginger,
  finely chopped
2 lemon grass stalks, finely chopped
2 shallots, finely chopped
15ml/1 tbsp tomato purée
250ml/8fl oz/1 cup coconut cream
4–6 kaffir lime leaves (optional)
15–30ml/1–2 tbsp fresh lime juice
15–30ml/1–2 tbsp fish sauce
1 cucumber, peeled, seeded and cut
  into 5cm/2in batons
1 tomato, seeded and cut into strips
2 red chillies, seeded and
  finely sliced
salt and freshly ground black pepper
2 spring onions, finely sliced, and
  a few coriander sprigs, to garnish

1 Cook the egg noodles in a saucepan of boiling water until just tender. Drain, rinse under cold running water and drain well.

2 Heat 15ml/1 tbsp of the oil in a large frying pan. Add the noodles, distributing them evenly, and fry for 4–5 minutes until crisp and golden. Turn the noodle cake over and fry the other side. Alternatively, make four individual cakes. Keep hot.

3 In a bowl, toss the prawns with the ground coriander, turmeric, garlic, ginger and lemon grass. Add salt and pepper to taste.

4 Heat the remaining oil in a large frying pan. Add the shallots, fry for 1 minute, then add the prawns and fry for 2 minutes more. Using a slotted spoon remove the prawns.

5 Stir the tomato purée and coconut cream into the mixture remaining in the pan. Stir in lime juice to taste and season with the fish sauce. Bring the sauce to a simmer, return the prawns to the sauce, then add the kaffir lime leaves, if using, and the cucumber. Simmer gently until the prawns are cooked and the sauce is reduced to a nice coating consistency.

6 Add the tomato, stir until just warmed through, then add the chillies. Serve on top of the crisp noodle cake(s), garnished with sliced spring onions and coriander sprigs.

Green Curry of Prawns

A popular fragrant creamy curry that also takes very little time to prepare. It can also be made with thin strips of chicken meat.

INGREDIENTS

Serves 4–6
30ml/2 tbsp vegetable oil
30ml/2 tbsp green curry paste
450g/1lb king prawns, shelled
  and deveined
4 kaffir lime leaves, torn
1 stalk lemon grass, bruised
  and chopped
250ml/8fl oz/1 cup coconut milk
30ml/2 tbsp fish sauce
½ cucumber, seeded and cut into thin
  batons
10–15 basil leaves
4 green chillies, sliced, to garnish

1 Heat the oil in a frying pan. Add the green curry paste and fry until bubbling and fragrant.

2 Add the prawns, kaffir lime leaves and lemon grass. Fry for 1–2 minutes, until the prawns are pink.

3 Stir in the coconut milk and bring to a gentle boil. Simmer, stirring occasionally, for about 5 minutes or until the prawns are tender.

4 Stir in the fish sauce, cucumber, and basil, then top with the green chillies and serve.

Chilli Prawns

This delightful, spicy combination makes a lovely, light main course for a casual supper. Serve with rice, noodles or even freshly cooked pasta and a leafy green salad.

INGREDIENTS

Serves 3–4

45ml/3 tbsp olive oil
2 shallots, chopped
2 garlic cloves, chopped
1 fresh red chilli, chopped
450g/1lb ripe tomatoes, skinned, seeded and chopped
15ml/1 tbsp tomato purée
1 bay leaf
1 thyme sprig
90ml/6 tbsp dry white wine
450g/1lb cooked large prawns, peeled
salt and ground black pepper
roughly torn basil leaves, to garnish

1 Heat the oil in a pan, then add the shallots, garlic and chilli and fry until the garlic starts to brown.

2 Add the tomatoes, tomato purée, bay leaf, thyme, wine and seasoning. Bring to the boil, then reduce the heat and cook gently for about 10 minutes, stirring occasionally, until the sauce has thickened. Discard the herbs.

3 Stir the prawns into the sauce and heat through for a few minutes. Taste and adjust the seasoning. Scatter over the basil leaves and serve at once.

COOK'S TIP

For a milder flavour, remove all the seeds from the chilli.

Scallops with Ginger

Scallops are at their best in the winter, but are available frozen throughout the year. Rich and creamy, this dish is very simple to make and utterly scrumptious.

INGREDIENTS

Serves 4

8–12 scallops, shelled
40g/1½oz/3 tbsp butter
2.5cm/1in fresh root ginger, finely chopped
1 bunch spring onions, sliced diagonally
60ml/4 tbsp white vermouth
250ml/8fl oz/1 cup crème fraîche
salt and ground black pepper
chopped fresh parsley, to garnish

1 Remove the tough muscle opposite the coral on each scallop. Separate the coral and cut the white part of the scallop in half horizontally.

2 Melt the butter in a frying pan. Add the scallops, including the corals, and sauté for about 2 minutes until lightly browned. Take care not to overcook the scallops as this will make them tough.

3 Lift out the scallops with a slotted spoon and transfer to a warmed serving dish. Keep warm.

4 Add the ginger and spring onions to the pan and stir-fry for 2 minutes. Pour in the vermouth and allow to bubble until it has almost evaporated. Stir in the crème fraîche and cook for a few minutes until the sauce has thickened. Taste and adjust the seasoning.

5 Pour the sauce over the scallops, sprinkle with parsley and serve immediately.

Baked Lobster with Black Beans

The term "baked", as used on most Chinese restaurant menus, is not strictly correct – "pot-roasted" or "pan-baked" is more accurate.

INGREDIENTS

Serves 4–6

1 large or 2 medium lobsters, about 800g/1¾lb in total
vegetable oil, for deep-frying
1 garlic clove, finely chopped
5ml/1 tsp finely chopped fresh root ginger
2–3 spring onions, chopped
30ml/2 tbsp black bean sauce
30ml/2 tbsp Chinese rice wine or dry sherry
120ml/4fl oz/½ cup stock or water
fresh coriander leaves, to garnish

1 Starting from the head, cut the lobster in half lengthways. Discard the legs, remove the claws and crack them with the back of a cleaver. Discard the feathery lungs and intestine. Cut each half into 4–5 pieces.

2 Heat the oil in a preheated wok and deep-fry the lobster pieces for about 2 minutes, or until the shells turn bright orange. Remove the pieces from the wok and drain on kitchen paper.

3 Pour off the excess oil, leaving about 15ml/1 tbsp in the wok. Add the garlic, ginger, spring onions and black bean sauce and stir-fry for 1 minute.

4 Add the lobster pieces to the sauce and blend well. Add the rice wine or dry sherry and stock, bring to the boil, cover and cook for 2–3 minutes. Serve garnished with coriander leaves.

COOK'S TIP

Ideally, buy live lobsters and cook them yourself. Ready-cooked ones have usually been boiled for far too long and have lost much of their delicate flavour and texture.

Lemon-grass-and-basil-scented Mussels

The classic Thai flavourings of lemon grass and basil are used in this fragrant dish.

INGREDIENTS

Serves 4

1.75kg/4–4½lb fresh mussels in
  their shells
2 lemon grass stalks
5–6 fresh basil sprigs
5cm/2in fresh root ginger
2 shallots, finely chopped
150ml/¼ pint/⅔ cup fish stock

1 Scrub the mussels under cold running water, scraping off any barnacles with a small, sharp knife. Pull or cut off the hairy "beards". Discard any mussels with damaged shells and any that remain open when they are sharply tapped.

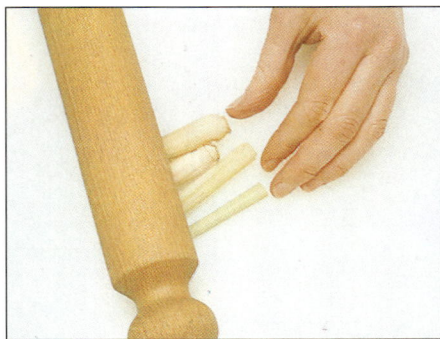

2 Cut each lemon grass stalk in half and bruise with a rolling pin.

3 Pull the basil leaves off the stems and roughly chop half of them. Reserve the remainder.

4 Put the mussels, lemon grass, chopped basil, ginger, shallots and stock in a wok. Bring to the boil, cover and simmer for 5 minutes. Discard the lemon grass and any mussels that remain closed, scatter over the reserved basil leaves and serve immediately.

MEAT & POULTRY DISHES

~

Pork and Vegetable Stir-fry

A quick and easy stir-fry of pork and a mixture of vegetables, this makes an excellent family lunch or supper dish.

INGREDIENTS

Serves 4
225g/8oz can pineapple chunks
15ml/1 tbsp cornflour
30ml/2 tbsp light soy sauce
15ml/1 tbsp Chinese rice wine or
  dry sherry
15ml/1 tbsp soft brown sugar
15ml/1 tbsp white wine vinegar
5ml/1 tsp Chinese five-spice powder
10ml/2 tsp olive oil
1 red onion, sliced
1 garlic clove, crushed
1 fresh red chilli, seeded and chopped
2.5cm/1in fresh root ginger
350g/12oz lean pork tenderloin, cut
  into thin strips
175g/6oz carrots
1 red pepper, seeded and sliced
175g/6oz mangetouts, halved
115g/4oz beansprouts
200g/7oz can sweetcorn kernels
30ml/2 tbsp chopped fresh coriander
salt
15ml/1 tbsp toasted sesame seeds,
  to garnish

1 Drain the pineapple, reserving the juice. In a small bowl, blend the cornflour with the reserved pineapple juice. Add the soy sauce, rice wine or dry sherry, sugar, vinegar and five-spice powder, stir to mix and set aside.

2 Heat the oil in a preheated wok or large, non-stick frying pan. Add the onion, garlic, chilli and ginger and stir-fry for 30 seconds. Add the pork and stir-fry for 2–3 minutes.

3 Cut the carrots into matchstick strips. Add to the wok with the red pepper and stir-fry for 2–3 minutes. Add the mangetouts, beansprouts and sweetcorn and stir-fry for 1–2 minutes.

4 Pour in the sauce mixture and the reserved pineapple and stir-fry until the sauce thickens. Reduce the heat and stir-fry for a further 1–2 minutes. Stir in the coriander and season to taste. Sprinkle with sesame seeds and serve immediately.

Thai Sweet-and-sour Pork

Sweet and sour is traditionally a Chinese creation but the Thais do it very well. This version has an altogether fresher and cleaner flavour and it makes a good one-dish meal when served over rice.

INGREDIENTS

Serves 4

350g/12oz lean pork
30ml/2 tbsp vegetable oil
4 garlic cloves, finely sliced
1 small red onion, sliced
30ml/2 tbsp fish sauce
15ml/1 tbsp granulated sugar
1 red pepper, seeded and diced
½ cucumber, seeded and sliced
2 plum tomatoes, cut into wedges
115g/4oz pineapple, cut into
  small chunks
freshly ground black pepper
2 spring onions, cut into short lengths
coriander leaves, to garnish
spring onions, shredded, to garnish

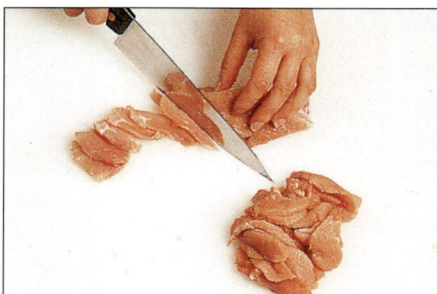

1 Slice the pork into thin strips. Heat the oil in a wok or large frying pan.

2 Add the garlic and fry until golden, then add the pork and stir-fry for about 4–5 minutes. Add the onion.

3 Season with fish sauce, sugar and freshly ground black pepper. Stir and cook for 3–4 minutes, or until the pork is cooked.

4 Add the rest of the vegetables, the pineapple and spring onions. You may need to add a few tablespoons of water. Continue to stir-fry for another 3–4 minutes. Serve hot garnished with coriander leaves and spring onion.

Crisp Pork Meatballs Laced with Noodles

These little meatballs, decoratively coated with a lacing of noodles, look very impressive, but are actually extremely easy to make.

INGREDIENTS

Serves 4

400g/14oz minced pork
2 garlic cloves, finely chopped
30ml/2 tbsp chopped fresh coriander
15ml/1 tbsp oyster sauce
30ml/2 tbsp fresh breadcrumbs
1 egg, beaten
175g/6oz fresh thin egg noodles
oil, for deep-frying
salt and ground black pepper
fresh coriander leaves, to garnish
spinach leaves and chilli sauce or
    tomato sauce, to serve

1 Mix together the pork, garlic, chopped coriander, oyster sauce, breadcrumbs and egg. Season with salt and pepper.

2 Knead the pork mixture until it is sticky, then form into balls about the size of a walnut.

3 Blanch the noodles in a saucepan of boiling water for 2–3 minutes. Drain, rinse under cold running water and drain well.

4 Wrap 3–5 strands of noodles securely around each meatball in a criss-cross pattern.

5 Heat the oil in a deep-fryer or preheated wok. Deep-fry the meatballs in batches until golden brown and cooked through to the centre. As each batch browns, remove with a slotted spoon and drain well on kitchen paper. Serve hot on a bed of spinach leaves, garnished with fresh coriander leaves and with chilli sauce or tomato sauce in a small dish.

Fragrant Thai Meatballs

INGREDIENTS

Serves 4–6

450g/1lb lean minced pork or beef
15ml/1 tbsp chopped garlic
1 stalk lemon grass, finely chopped
4 spring onions, finely chopped
15ml/1 tbsp chopped fresh coriander
30ml/2 tbsp red curry paste
15ml/1 tbsp lemon juice
15ml/1 tbsp fish sauce
1 egg
salt and freshly ground black pepper
rice flour for dusting
oil for frying
sprigs of coriander, to garnish

For the peanut sauce

15ml/1 tbsp vegetable oil
15ml/1 tbsp red curry paste
30ml/2 tbsp crunchy peanut butter
15ml/1 tbsp palm sugar
15ml/1 tbsp lemon juice
250ml/8fl oz/1 cup coconut milk

1 Make the peanut sauce. Heat the oil in a small saucepan, add the curry paste and fry for 1 minute.

2 Stir in the rest of the ingredients and bring to the boil. Lower the heat and simmer for 5 minutes, until the sauce thickens.

3 Make the meatballs. Combine all the ingredients except for the rice flour, oil and coriander, and add some seasoning. Mix and blend everything together well.

4 Roll and shape the meat into small balls about the size of a walnut. Dust the meatballs with rice flour.

5 Heat the oil in a wok until hot and deep fry the meatballs in batches until nicely browned and cooked through. Drain on kitchen paper. Serve garnished with sprigs of coriander and accompanied with the peanut sauce.

Stuffed Thai Omelette

INGREDIENTS

Serves 4

30ml/2 tbsp vegetable oil
2 garlic cloves, finely chopped
1 small onion, finely chopped
225g/8oz minced pork
30ml/2 tbsp fish sauce
5ml/1 tsp granulated sugar
freshly ground black pepper
2 tomatoes, peeled and chopped
15ml/1 tbsp chopped fresh coriander

For the omelette

5–6 eggs
15ml/1 tbsp fish sauce
30ml/2 tbsp vegetable oil
sprigs of coriander, to garnish
red chillies, sliced, to garnish

1 First heat the oil in a wok or frying pan. Add the garlic and onion and fry for 3–4 minutes until softened. Stir in the pork and fry for about 7–10 minutes, until lightly browned.

2 Add the fish sauce, sugar, freshly ground pepper and tomatoes. Stir to combine and simmer until the sauce thickens slightly. Mix in the chopped fresh coriander.

3 To make the omelettes, whisk together the eggs and fish sauce.

4 Heat 15ml/1 tbsp of the oil in an omelette pan or wok. Add half the beaten egg and tilt the pan to spread the egg into a thin even sheet.

5 When set, spoon half the filling over the centre of the omelette. Fold in opposite sides; first the top and bottom, then the right and left sides to make a neat square parcel.

6 Slide out on to a warm serving dish, folded-side down. Repeat with the rest of the oil, eggs and filling. Serve garnished with sprigs of coriander and red chillies.

Beef Stir-fry with Crisp Parsnips

Wonderful crisp shreds of parsnip add extra crunchiness to this unusual stir-fry – a great supper dish to share with friends.

INGREDIENTS

Serves 4

350g/12oz parsnips
450g/1lb rump steak
450g/1lb trimmed leeks
2 red peppers, seeded
350g/12oz courgettes
90ml/6 tbsp vegetable oil
2 garlic cloves, crushed
45ml/3 tbsp hoisin sauce
salt and ground black pepper

1 Peel the parsnips and cut in half lengthways. Place the flat surface on a chopping board and cut them into thin strips. Finely shred each piece. Rinse in cold water and drain thoroughly. Dry the parsnips on kitchen paper, if necessary.

2 Cut the steak into thin strips. Split the leeks in half lengthways and thickly slice at an angle. Roughly chop the peppers and thinly slice the courgettes.

3 Heat the oil in a preheated wok or large frying pan. Fry the parsnips until crisp and golden. You may need to do this in batches, adding a little more oil if necessary. Remove with a slotted spoon and drain on kitchen paper.

4 Stir-fry the steak in the wok or frying pan until golden and cooked through. You may need to do this in batches, adding more oil if necessary. Remove and drain on kitchen paper.

5 Stir-fry the garlic, leeks, peppers and courgettes for about 10 minutes, or until golden brown and beginning to soften but still retaining a little bite. Season the mixture well.

6 Return the meat to the pan with the hoisin sauce. Stir-fry for 2–3 minutes, or until piping hot. Adjust the seasoning and serve with the crisp parsnips piled on top.

Stir-fried Beef with Mangetouts

The crisp texture and fresh taste of mangetouts perfectly complement the melt-in-the-mouth tenderness of the steak, all served in a richly aromatic sauce.

INGREDIENTS

Serves 4

450g/1lb rump steak
45ml/3 tbsp soy sauce
30ml/2 tbsp Chinese rice wine or dry sherry
15ml/1 tbsp soft brown sugar
2.5ml/½ tsp cornflour
15ml/1 tbsp vegetable oil
15ml/1 tbsp finely chopped fresh root ginger
15ml/1 tbsp finely chopped garlic
225g/8oz mangetouts

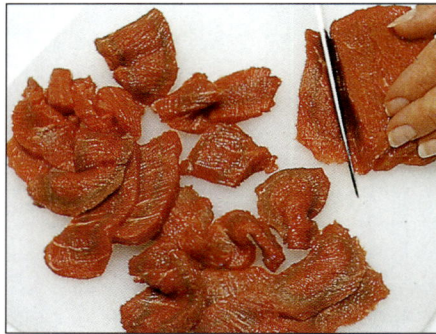

1 Cut the steak into even-sized, very thin strips.

2 Combine the soy sauce, rice wine or dry sherry, brown sugar and cornflour. Mix well and set aside.

3 Heat the oil in a preheated wok. Add the ginger and garlic and stir-fry for 30 seconds. Add the steak and stir-fry for 2 minutes, or until evenly browned.

4 Add the mangetouts and stir-fry for a further 3 minutes.

5 Stir the soy sauce mixture until smooth, then add to the wok. Bring to the boil, stirring constantly, lower the heat and simmer until the sauce is thick and smooth. Serve immediately.

Green Beef Curry with Thai Aubergine

This is a very quick curry so be sure to use good quality meat.

INGREDIENTS

Serves 4–6

15ml/1 tbsp vegetable oil
45ml/3 tbsp green curry paste
600ml/1 pint/2½ cups coconut milk
450g/1lb beef sirloin
4 kaffir lime leaves, torn
15–30ml/1–2 tbsp fish sauce
5ml/1 tsp palm sugar
150g/5oz small Thai aubergines, halved
a small handful of Thai basil
2 green chillies, to garnish

For the green curry paste

15 hot green chillies
2 stalks lemon grass, chopped
3 shallots, sliced
2 garlic cloves
15ml/1 tbsp chopped galangal
4 kaffir lime leaves, chopped
2.5ml/½ tsp grated kaffir lime rind
5ml/1 tsp chopped coriander root
6 black peppercorns
5ml/1 tsp coriander seeds, roasted
5ml/1 tsp cumin seeds, roasted
15ml/1 tbsp sugar
5ml/1 tsp salt
5ml/1 tsp shrimp paste (optional)

1 Make the green curry paste. Combine all the ingredients, except for the oil. Pound in a pestle and mortar or process in a food processor until smooth. Add the oil a little at a time and blend well between each addition. Keep in a glass jar in the fridge until required.

2 Heat the oil in a large saucepan or wok. Add 45ml/3 tbsp curry paste and fry until fragrant.

3 Stir in half the coconut milk, a little at a time. Cook for about 5–6 minutes, until an oily sheen appears.

4 Cut the beef into long thin slices and add to the saucepan with the kaffir lime leaves, fish sauce, sugar and aubergines. Cook for 2–3 minutes, then stir in the remaining coconut milk.

5 Bring back to a simmer and cook until the meat and aubergines are tender. Stir in the Thai basil just before serving. Finely shred the green chillies and use to garnish the curry.

Thick Beef Curry in Sweet Peanut Sauce

This curry is deliciously rich and thicker than most other Thai curries. Serve with boiled jasmine rice and salted duck's eggs, if liked.

INGREDIENTS

Serves 4–6

600ml/1 pint/2½ cups coconut milk
45ml/3 tbsp red curry paste
45ml/3 tbsp fish sauce
30ml/2 tbsp palm sugar
2 stalks lemon grass, bruised
450g/1lb rump steak, cut into
  thin strips
75g/3oz roasted ground peanuts
2 red chillies, sliced
5 kaffir lime leaves, torn
salt and freshly ground black pepper
2 salted eggs, to serve
10–15 Thai basil leaves, to garnish

1 Put half the coconut milk into a heavy-bottomed saucepan and heat, stirring, until it boils and separates.

— COOK'S TIP —

If you don't have the time to make your own red curry paste, you can buy a ready-made Thai curry paste. There is a wide range available in most supermarkets.

2 Add the red curry paste and cook until fragrant. Add the fish sauce, palm sugar and lemon grass.

3 Continue to cook until the colour deepens. Add the rest of the coconut milk. Bring back to the boil.

4 Add the beef and ground peanuts. Stir and cook for 8–10 minutes or until most of the liquid has evaporated.

5 Add the chillies and kaffir lime leaves. Adjust the seasoning to taste. Serve with salted eggs and garnish with Thai basil leaves.

Sukiyaki Beef

This Japanese dish, with its mixture of meat, vegetables, noodles and tofu, is a meal in itself. If you want to do it properly, eat the meal with chopsticks and then use a spoon to collect the stock juices.

INGREDIENTS

Serves 4
450g/1lb thick rump steak
200g/7oz Japanese rice noodles
15ml/1 tbsp shredded suet
200g/7oz firm tofu, cut into cubes
8 shiitake mushrooms, hard stems trimmed
2 medium leeks, sliced into 2.5cm/1in lengths
90g/3½oz baby spinach, to serve

For the stock
15ml/1 tbsp caster sugar
90ml/6 tbsp sake, Chinese rice wine or dry sherry
45ml/3 tbsp dark soy sauce
120ml/4fl oz/½ cup water

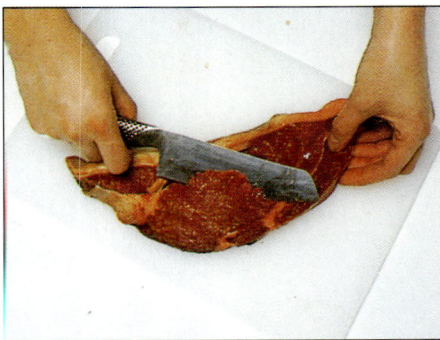

1 Cut the steak into thin slices using a cleaver or sharp knife.

2 Blanch the noodles in boiling water for 2 minutes. Drain thoroughly and set aside.

3 Make the stock: mix together the sugar, sake, rice wine or dry sherry, soy sauce and water.

4 Melt the suet in a preheated wok. Add the steak and stir-fry for 2–3 minutes, or until cooked through but still pink.

5 Pour the stock over the beef.

6 Add the tofu, mushrooms and leeks and cook for 4 minutes, or until the leeks are tender. Serve a selection of the different ingredients, together with a few baby spinach leaves, to each person.

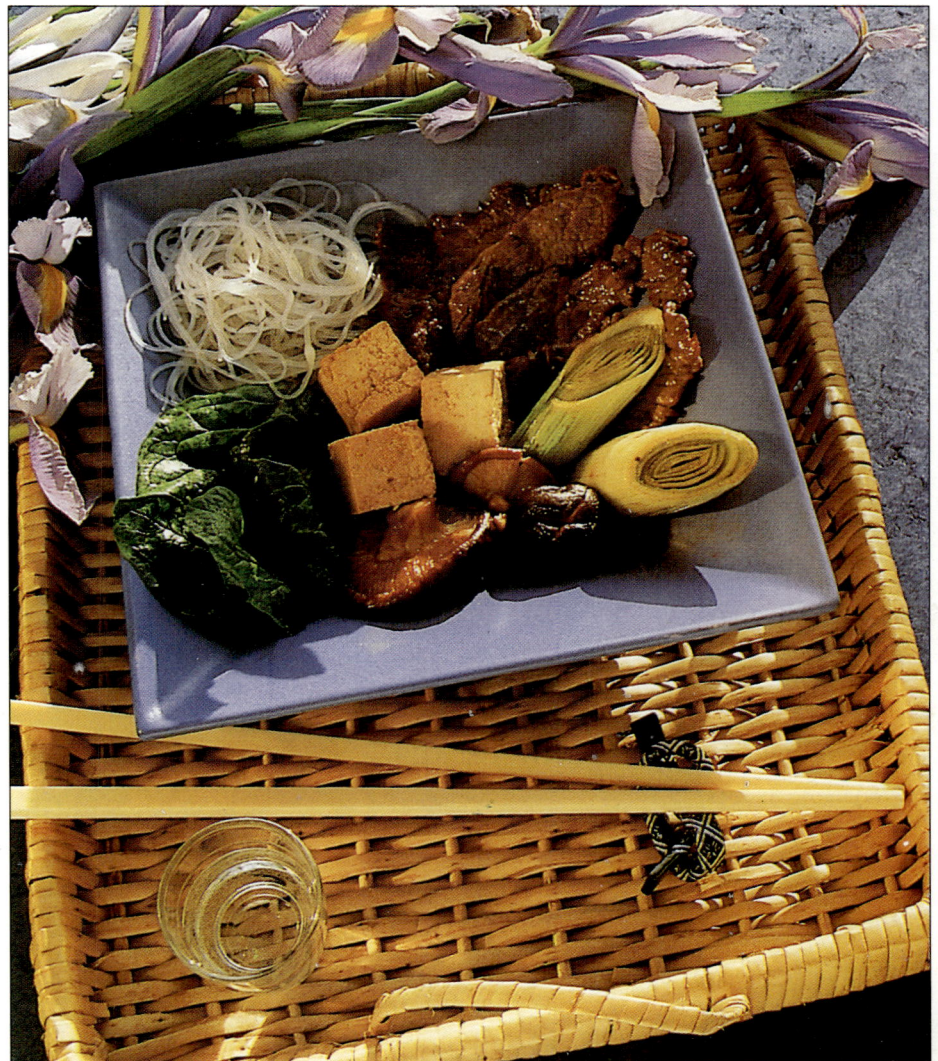

Don't USE!

Indonesian-style Satay Chicken

Satay traditionally forms part of a *Rijsttafel* – literally rice table – a vast feast of as many as 40 different dishes served with a large bowl of plain rice. However, for the less ambitious, creamy coconut satay makes these chicken pieces a mouth-watering dish to present at the table at any time of the day.

INGREDIENTS

Serves 4

50g/2oz raw peanuts
45ml/3 tbsp vegetable oil
1 small onion, finely chopped
2.5cm/1in fresh root ginger, peeled and finely chopped
1 clove garlic, crushed
675g/1½lb chicken thighs, skinned and cut into cubes
90g/3½oz creamed coconut, roughly chopped
15ml/1 tbsp chilli sauce
60ml/4 tbsp crunchy peanut butter
5ml/1 tsp soft dark brown sugar
150ml/¼ pint/⅔ cup milk
1.5ml/¼ tsp salt

1 Shell the peanuts and remove the skins by rubbing them between the palms of the hands. Put them in a small bowl, add just enough water to cover and soak for 1 minute. Drain the nuts and cut them into slivers.

2 Heat the wok and add 5ml/1 tsp oil. When the oil is hot, stir-fry the peanuts for 1 minute until crisp and golden. Remove with a slotted spoon and drain on kitchen paper.

3 Add the remaining oil to the hot wok. When the oil is hot, add the onion, ginger and garlic and stir-fry for 2–3 minutes until softened but not browned. Remove with a slotted spoon and drain on kitchen paper.

--- COOK'S TIP ---

Soak bamboo skewers in cold water for at least 2 hours, or preferably overnight, so that they do not char when keeping the threaded chicken warm in the oven.

4 Add the chicken pieces to the wok and stir-fry for 3–4 minutes until crisp and golden on all sides. Thread on to pre-soaked bamboo skewers and keep warm.

5 Add the creamed coconut to the hot wok in small pieces and stir-fry until melted. Add the chilli sauce, peanut butter and ginger mixture and simmer for 2 minutes. Stir in the sugar, milk and salt, and simmer for a further 3 minutes. Serve the skewered chicken hot, with a dish of the hot dipping sauce sprinkled with the roasted peanuts.

Stir-fried Sweet-and-sour Chicken

This all-in-one stir-fry has a South-east Asian influence, and it is ideal for today's cook who is so often short of time.

INGREDIENTS

Serves 4

275g/10oz Chinese egg noodles
30ml/2 tbsp vegetable oil
3 spring onions, chopped
1 garlic clove, crushed
2.5cm/1in fresh root ginger, peeled and grated
5ml/1 tsp hot paprika
5ml/1 tsp ground coriander
3 chicken breast fillets, sliced
115g/4oz sugar snap peas, topped and tailed
115g/4oz baby sweetcorn, halved
225g/8oz fresh beansprouts
15ml/1 tbsp cornflour
45ml/3 tbsp soy sauce
45ml/3 tbsp lemon juice
15ml/1 tbsp sugar
salt
45ml/3 tbsp chopped fresh coriander or spring onion tops, to garnish

1 Bring a large saucepan of salted water to the boil. Add the noodles and cook according to the packet instructions if using dried noodles. If using fresh egg noodles, cook for a few minutes only, stirring occasionally to separate. Drain thoroughly, cover and keep warm.

2 Heat the oil in a pre-heated wok. Add the spring onions and cook over a gentle heat. Mix in the garlic, ginger, paprika, coriander and chicken, then stir-fry for 3–4 minutes.

3 Add the peas, baby sweetcorn and beansprouts, cover and cook briefly. Add the noodles.

4 Combine the cornflour, soy sauce, lemon juice and sugar in a small bowl. Add to the wok and simmer briefly to thicken. Serve immediately, garnished with chopped coriander or spring onion tops.

COOK'S TIP

Large wok lids are cumbersome and can be difficult to store in a small kitchen. Consider placing a circle of greaseproof paper against the food surface to keep the cooking juices in.

Stir-fried Chicken with Basil and Chillies

This quick and easy chicken dish is an excellent introduction to Thai cuisine. Deep frying the basil adds another dimension to this dish. Thai basil, which is sometimes known as Holy basil, has a unique, pungent flavour that is both spicy and sharp. The dull leaves have serrated edges.

INGREDIENTS

Serves 4–6
45ml/3 tbsp vegetable oil
4 garlic cloves, sliced
2–4 red chillies, seeded and chopped
450g/1lb chicken, cut into
  bite-size pieces
30–45ml/2–3 tbsp fish sauce
10ml/2 tsp dark soy sauce
5ml/1 tsp sugar
10–12 Thai basil leaves
2 red chillies, finely sliced, to garnish
20 Thai basil leaves, deep fried
  (optional)

1 Heat the oil in a wok or large frying pan and swirl it around.

2 Add the garlic and chillies and stir-fry until golden.

3 Add the chicken and stir-fry until it changes colour.

4 Season with fish sauce, soy sauce and sugar. Continue to stir-fry for 3-4 minutes or until the chicken is cooked. Stir in the fresh Thai basil leaves. Garnish with sliced chillies and the deep fried basil, if using.

--- COOK'S TIP ---

To deep fry Thai basil leaves, make sure that the leaves are completely dry. Deep fry in hot oil for about 30–40 seconds, lift out and drain on kitchen paper.

Gingered Chicken Noodles

A blend of ginger, spices and coconut milk flavours this delicious supper dish, which is made in minutes. For a real oriental touch, add a little fish sauce to taste, just before serving.

INGREDIENTS

Serves 4

350g/12oz boneless chicken breasts, skinned
225g/8oz courgettes
275g/10oz aubergine
30ml/2 tbsp vegetable oil
5cm/2in fresh root ginger, finely chopped
6 spring onions, sliced
10ml/2 tsp Thai green curry paste
400ml/14fl oz/1⅔ cups coconut milk
475ml/16fl oz/2 cups chicken stock
115g/4oz medium egg noodles
45ml/3 tbsp chopped fresh coriander
15ml/1 tbsp lemon juice
salt and ground black pepper
chopped fresh coriander, to garnish

1 Cut the chicken into bite-sized pieces. Halve the courgettes lengthways and roughly chop them. Roughly chop the aubergine.

2 Heat the oil in a large saucepan and cook the chicken until golden. Remove with a slotted spoon and drain on kitchen paper.

3 Add a little more oil, if necessary, and cook the ginger and spring onions for 3 minutes. Add the courgettes and cook for 2–3 minutes, or until beginning to turn golden. Stir in the Thai curry paste and cook for 1 minute.

4 Add the coconut milk, stock, aubergine and chicken and simmer for 10 minutes. Add the noodles and cook for a further 5 minutes, or until the chicken is cooked and the noodles are tender. Stir in the coriander and lemon juice and adjust the seasoning. Serve immediately garnished with chopped fresh coriander.

Szechuan Chicken

A wok is the ideal cooking pot for this stir-fried chicken dish. The flavours emerge wonderfully and the chicken is fresh and crisp.

INGREDIENTS

Serves 4

350g/12oz chicken thigh, boned and skinned
1.5ml/¼ tsp salt
½ egg white, lightly beaten
10ml/2 tsp cornflour paste
1 green pepper, cored and seeded
60ml/4 tbsp vegetable oil
3–4 whole dried red chillies, soaked in water for 10 minutes
1 spring onion, cut into short sections
few small pieces of fresh root ginger, peeled
15ml/1 tbsp sweet bean paste or hoi-sin sauce
5ml/1 tsp chilli bean paste
15ml/1 tbsp Chinese rice wine or dry sherry
115g/4oz roasted cashew nuts
few drops sesame oil

1 Cut the chicken meat into small cubes, each about the size of a sugar lump. Mix together the chicken, salt, egg white and cornflour paste in a bowl.

2 Cut the green pepper into cubes about the same size as the chicken.

3 Heat the oil in a preheated wok. Stir-fry the chicken cubes for about 1 minute, or until the colour changes. Remove from the wok with a slotted spoon and keep warm.

4 Add the green pepper, chillies, spring onion and ginger and stir-fry for about 1 minute. Then add the chicken, sweet bean paste or hoi-sin sauce, chilli bean paste and rice wine or sherry. Blend well and cook for 1 minute more. Finally add the cashew nuts and sesame oil. Serve hot.

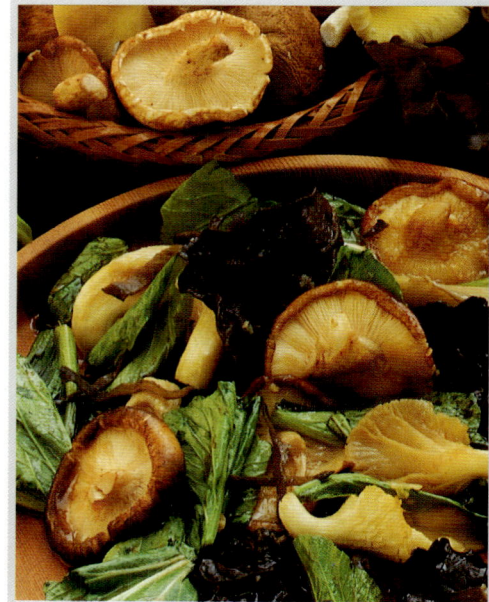

VEGETABLES
& VEGETARIAN
DISHES

~

Stir-fried Mixed Vegetables

When selecting different items for a stir-fried dish, never mix the ingredients indiscriminately. The idea is to achieve a harmonious balance of colour and texture.

INGREDIENTS

Serves 4
225g/8oz Chinese leaves
115g/4oz baby corn cobs
115g/4oz broccoli
1 medium or 2 small carrots
60ml/4 tbsp vegetable oil
5ml/1 tsp salt
5ml/1 tsp light brown sugar
vegetable stock or water, if necessary
15ml/1 tbsp light soy sauce
few drops of sesame oil (optional)

1 Cut the vegetables into roughly similar shapes and sizes.

2 Heat the oil in a preheated wok and stir-fry the vegetables for about 2 minutes.

3 Add the salt and sugar and a little stock or water, if necessary, and continue stirring for another minute. Add the soy sauce and sesame oil, if using. Blend well and serve.

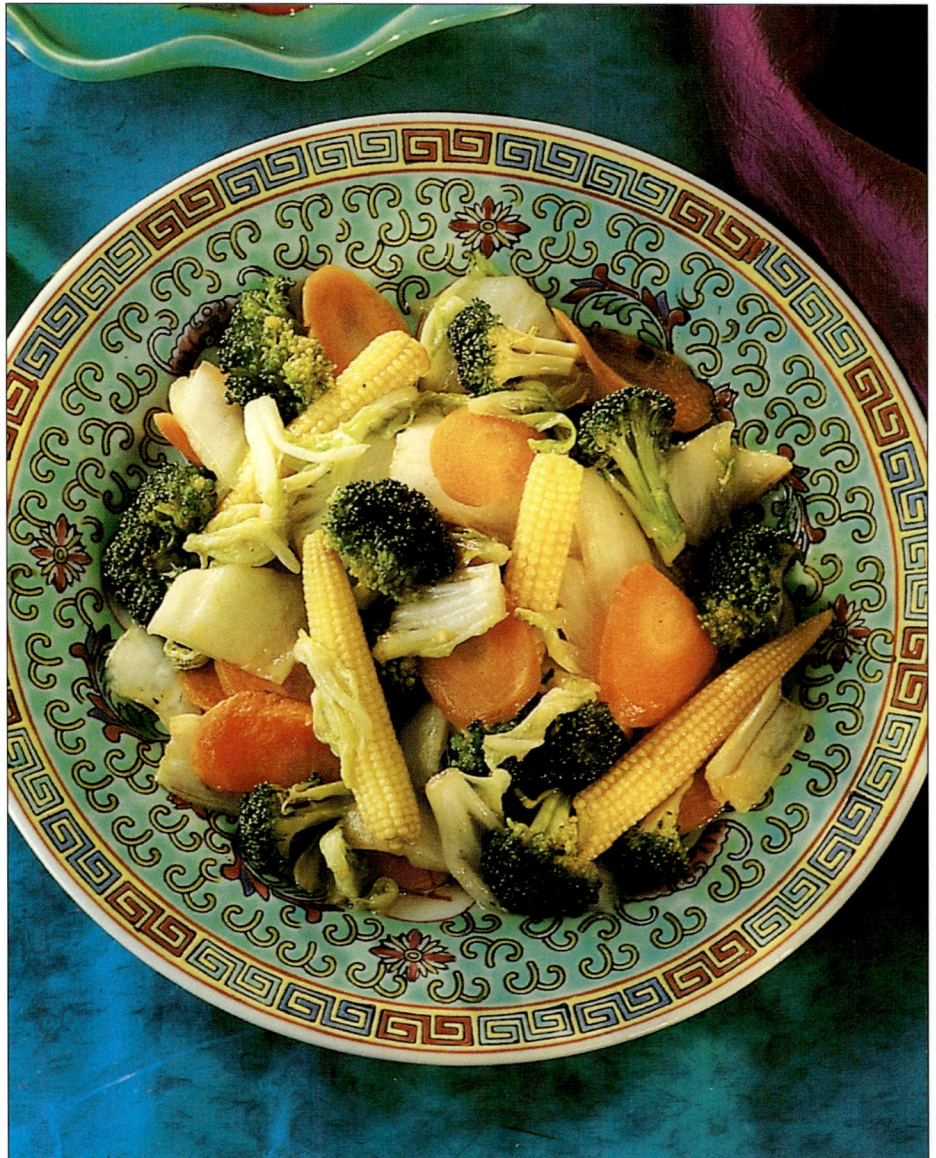

Pak Choi and Mushroom Stir-fry

Try to buy all the varieties of mushroom for this dish – wild oyster and shiitake mushrooms have particularly distinctive, delicate flavours that work well when stir-fried.

INGREDIENTS

Serves 4
4 dried black Chinese mushrooms
150ml/¼ pint/⅔ cup hot water
450g/1lb pak choi
50g/2oz oyster mushrooms,
    preferably wild
50g/2oz shiitake mushrooms
15ml/1 tbsp vegetable oil
1 clove garlic, crushed
30ml/2 tbsp oyster sauce

1 Soak the black Chinese mushrooms in the hot water for 15 minutes to soften.

COOK'S TIP

Pak choi, also called bok choi, pok choi and spoon cabbage, is an attractive member of the cabbage family, with long, smooth white stems and dark green leaves. It has a pleasant flavour which does not, in any way, resemble that of cabbage.

---

2 Tear the pak choi into bite-sized pieces with your fingers.

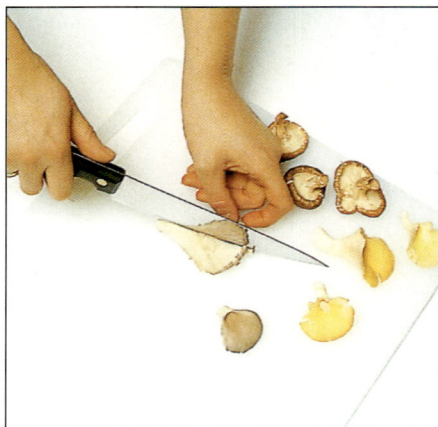

3 Halve any large oyster and shiitake mushrooms, using a sharp knife.

4 Strain the Chinese mushrooms. Heat the wok, then add the oil. When the oil is hot, stir-fry the garlic until softened but not coloured.

5 Add the pak choi to the wok and stir-fry for 1 minute. Mix in all the mushrooms and stir-fry for 1 minute.

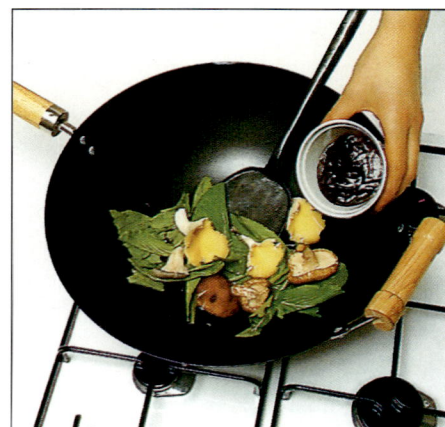

6 Add the oyster sauce, toss well and serve immediately.

Mooli, Beetroot and Carrot Stir-fry

This is a dazzlingly colourful dish with a crunchy texture and fragrant taste.

INGREDIENTS

Serves 4
25g/1oz/¼ cup pine nuts
115g/4oz mooli, peeled
115g/4oz raw beetroot, peeled
115g/4oz carrots, peeled
25ml/1½ tbsp vegetable oil
juice of 1 orange
30ml/2 tbsp chopped fresh coriander
salt and ground black pepper

1 Place the pine nuts in a preheated wok and toss until golden brown. Remove and set aside.

2 Cut the mooli, beetroot and carrots into long, thin strips.

3 Heat the oil in a preheated wok. When the oil is hot, stir-fry the mooli, raw beetroot and carrots for 2–3 minutes. Remove the vegetables from the wok and set aside.

4 Pour the orange juice into the wok and simmer for 2 minutes. Remove and keep warm.

5 Arrange the vegetables attractively on a warmed platter, sprinkle over the coriander and season to taste with salt and pepper.

6 Drizzle over the orange juice, sprinkle with the pine nuts, and serve immediately.

Chinese Sprouts

If you are bored with plain boiled Brussels sprouts, try pepping them up with this unusual stir-fried method, which uses the minimum of oil.

INGREDIENTS

Serves 4
450g/1lb Brussels sprouts
5ml/1 tsp sesame or sunflower oil
2 spring onions, sliced
2.5ml/½ tsp Chinese five-spice powder
15ml/1 tbsp light soy sauce

1 Trim the Brussels sprouts, then shred them finely using a large sharp knife or shred in a food processor.

2 Heat the oil in a preheated wok or frying pan and add the sprouts and onions, then stir-fry for 2 minutes, without browning.

3 Stir in the five-spice powder and soy sauce, then cook, stirring, for a further 2–3 minutes, until just tender.

4 Serve hot, with grilled meat or fish or with Chinese dishes.

COOK'S TIP

Brussels sprouts are rich in vitamin C, and this is a good way to cook them to preserve the nutrients. Larger sprouts cook particularly well by this method, and cabbage can be cooked in the same way.

Indonesian Potatoes with Onions and Chilli Sauce

This adds another dimension to potato chips, with the addition of crisply fried onions and a hot soy sauce and chilli dressing. Eat *Kentang Gula* hot, warm or cold, as a tasty snack.

INGREDIENTS

Serves 6
3 large potatoes, about 225g/8oz each, peeled and cut into chips
sunflower or groundnut oil for deep-frying
2 onions, finely sliced
salt

For the dressing
1–2 fresh red chillies, seeded and ground
45ml/3 tbsp dark soy sauce

1 Rinse the potato chips and then pat dry very well with kitchen paper. Heat the oil and deep-fry the chips, until they are golden brown in colour and crisp.

2 Put the chips in a dish, sprinkle with salt and keep warm. Fry the onion slices in the hot oil until they are similarly crisp and golden brown. Drain well on kitchen paper and then add to the potato chips.

3 Mix the chillies with the soy sauce and heat gently.

4 Pour over the potato and onion mixture and serve as suggested.

VARIATION

Alternatively, boil the potatoes in their skins. Drain, cool and slice them and then shallow-fry until golden. Cook the onions and pour over the dressing, as above.

Courgettes with Noodles

Any courgette or member of the squash family can be used in this *Oseng Oseng,* which is very similar to a dish enjoyed in Malaysia, whose cuisine has strong links with Indonesia.

INGREDIENTS

Serves 4–6
450g/1lb courgettes, sliced
1 onion, finely sliced
1 garlic clove, finely chopped
30ml/2 tbsp sunflower oil
2.5ml/½ tsp ground turmeric
2 tomatoes, chopped
45ml/3 tbsp water
115g/4oz cooked, peeled prawns (optional)
25g/1oz cellophane noodles
salt

1 Use a potato peeler to cut thin strips from the outside of each courgette. Cut them in neat slices. Set the courgettes on one side. Fry the onion and garlic in hot oil; do not allow to brown.

2 Add the turmeric, courgette slices, chopped tomatoes, water and prawns, if using.

3 Put the noodles in a pan and pour over boiling water to cover, leave for a minute and then drain. Cut the noodles in 5cm/2in lengths and add to the vegetables.

4 Cover with a lid and cook in their own steam for 2–3 minutes. Toss everything well together. Season with salt to taste and serve while still hot.

Spiced Vegetables with Coconut

This spicy and substantial stir-fry could be served as a starter, or as a vegetarian main course for two. Eat it with spoons and forks, and provide hunks of granary bread for mopping up the delicious coconut milk.

INGREDIENTS

Serves 2–4

1 red chilli
1 bulb fennel
2 large carrots
6 celery sticks
30ml/2 tbsp grapeseed oil
2.5cm/1in fresh root ginger, peeled and grated
1 clove garlic, crushed
3 spring onions, sliced
1 x 400ml/14fl oz can thin coconut milk
15ml/1 tbsp chopped fresh coriander
salt and ground black pepper
fresh coriander sprigs, to garnish

COOK'S TIP

When buying fennel, look for well-rounded bulbs; flatter ones are immature and will not have developed their full aniseed-like flavour. The bulbs should be white with overlapping ridged layers. Avoid any that look damaged or bruised. The fennel should be dry, but not desiccated.

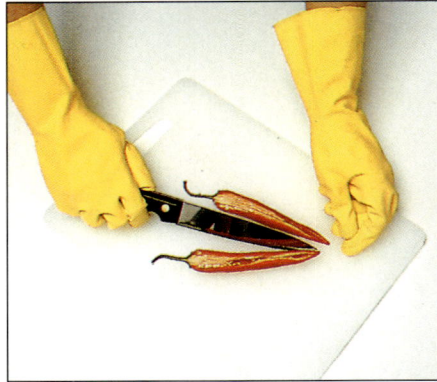

---

1 Halve, seed and finely chop the chilli. If necessary, wear rubber gloves to protect your hands.

2 Thinly slice the carrots and the celery sticks on the diagonal.

3 Trim the fennel bulb and slice roughly, using a sharp knife.

4 Heat the wok, then add the oil. When the oil is hot, add the chilli, fennel, carrots, celery, ginger, garlic and spring onions and stir-fry for 2 minutes.

5 Stir in the coconut milk with a large spoon and bring to the boil.

6 Stir in the coriander and salt and pepper, and serve garnished with coriander sprigs.

Bamboo Shoots and Chinese Mushrooms

Another name for this dish is "twin winter vegetables" because both bamboo shoots and mushrooms are at their best then. For that reason, try using canned winter bamboo shoots and extra "fat" mushrooms.

INGREDIENTS

Serves 4
50g/2oz dried Chinese mushrooms
275g/10oz can winter
 bamboo shoots
45ml/3 tbsp vegetable oil
1 spring onion, cut into
 short sections
30ml/2 tbsp light soy sauce or oyster
 sauce
15ml/1 tbsp Chinese rice wine or
 dry sherry
2.5ml/½ tsp light brown sugar
10ml/2 tsp cornflour paste
few drops sesame oil

1 Soak the mushrooms in cold water for at least 3 hours. Squeeze dry and discard any hard stalks, reserving the water. Cut the mushrooms in half or in quarters if they are large – keep them whole if small.

2 Rinse and drain the bamboo shoots, then cut them into small, wedge-shaped pieces.

3 Heat the oil in a preheated wok and stir-fry the mushrooms and bamboo shoots for about 1 minute. Add the spring onion, soy or oyster sauce, rice wine or sherry and the sugar, with about 2–3 tbsp of the reserved mushroom soaking liquid. Bring to the boil and braise for a further 1–2 minutes. Stir in the cornflour paste to thicken, sprinkle with the sesame oil and serve at once.

Stir-fried Tomatoes, Cucumber and Eggs

The cucumber can be replaced by a green pepper or courgettes if you prefer.

INGREDIENTS

Serves 4
175g/6oz firm tomatoes, skinned
½ cucumber, unpeeled
4 eggs
5ml/1 tsp salt
1 spring onion, finely chopped
60ml/4 tbsp vegetable oil
10ml/2 tsp Chinese rice wine or dry
 sherry (optional)

1 Cut the tomatoes and cucumber in half, then cut across into small wedges. In a bowl, beat the eggs with a pinch of salt and a few pieces of the chopped spring onion.

2 Heat about half the oil in a preheated wok, then pour in the eggs and scramble lightly over a moderate heat until set, but not too dry. Remove the scrambled egg from the wok and keep warm.

3 Add the remaining oil to the wok and heat over a high heat. Add the vegetables and stir-fry for 1 minute. Add the remaining salt, then the scrambled eggs and wine or sherry if using. Serve at once.

Tofu and Green Bean Red Curry

This is another curry that is simple and quick to make. This recipe uses green beans, but you can use almost any kind of vegetable such as aubergines, bamboo shoots or broccoli.

INGREDIENTS

Serves 4–6

600ml/1 pint/2½ cups coconut milk
15ml/1 tbsp red curry paste
45ml/3 tbsp fish sauce
10ml/2 tsp palm sugar
225g/8oz button mushrooms
115g/4oz green beans, trimmed
175g/6oz tofu, rinsed and cut into
  2cm/¾in cubes
4 kaffir lime leaves, torn
2 red chillies, sliced
coriander leaves, to garnish

1 Put about one third of the coconut milk in a wok or saucepan. Cook until it starts to separate and an oily sheen appears.

2 Add the red curry paste, fish sauce and sugar to the coconut milk. Mix together thoroughly.

3 Add the mushrooms. Stir and cook for 1 minute.

4 Stir in the rest of the coconut milk and bring back to the boil.

5 Add the green beans and cubes of tofu and simmer gently for another 4–5 minutes.

6 Stir in kaffir lime leaves and chillies. Serve garnished with the coriander leaves.

Pak Choi with Lime Dressing

For this Thai recipe, the coconut dressing is traditionally made using fish sauce, but vegetarians could use mushroom sauce instead. Beware, the red chillies make this a fiery dish!

INGREDIENTS

Serves 4
6 spring onions
2 pak choi
30ml/2 tbsp oil
3 fresh red chillies, cut into thin strips
4 garlic cloves, thinly sliced
15ml/1 tbsp crushed peanuts

For the dressing
15–30ml/1–2 tbsp fish sauce
30ml/2 tbsp lime juice
250ml/8fl oz/1 cup coconut milk

1 To make the dressing, blend together the fish sauce and lime juice, then stir in the coconut milk.

2 Trim the spring onions, then cut diagonally into slices, including all but the very tips of the green parts, but keeping the green and white parts separate.

3 Using a large sharp knife, cut the pak choi into very fine shreds.

4 Heat the oil in a preheated wok and stir-fry the chillies for 2–3 minutes until crisp. Transfer to a plate using a slotted spoon. Stir-fry the garlic for 30–60 seconds until golden brown and transfer to the plate with the chillies. Stir-fry the white parts of the spring onions for about 2–3 minutes and then add the green parts and stir-fry for a further 1 minute. Add to the plate with the chillies and garlic.

5 Bring a large pan of salted water to the boil and add the pak choi. Stir twice and then drain immediately. Place the warmed pak choi in a large bowl, add the coconut dressing and stir well. Spoon into a large serving bowl and sprinkle with the crushed peanuts and the stir-fried chilli mixture. Serve immediately.

Stir-fried Vegetables with Coriander Omelette

A wok is the ideal utensil for cooking an omelette as the heat is evenly distributed over the wide surface. This is a great supper dish for vegetarians. The glaze is intended to give the vegetables an appealing shine and does not constitute a sauce.

INGREDIENTS

Serves 3–4

For the omelette

2 eggs
30ml/2 tbsp water
45ml/3 tbsp chopped fresh coriander
salt and ground black pepper
15ml/1 tbsp groundnut oil

For the glazed vegetables

15ml/1 tbsp cornflour
30ml/2 tbsp dry sherry
15ml/1 tbsp sweet chilli sauce
120ml/4 fl oz/½ cup vegetable stock
30ml/2 tbsp groundnut oil
5ml/1 tsp grated fresh root ginger
6–8 spring onions, sliced
115g/4oz mangetouts
1 yellow pepper, seeded and sliced
115g/4oz fresh shiitake or
  button mushrooms
115g/4oz canned water chestnuts,
  drained and rinsed
115g/4oz beansprouts
½ small Chinese cabbage,
  roughly shredded

--- COOK'S TIP ---

Vary the combination of vegetables used according to availability and taste, but make sure that you slice or chop them to approximately the same size and thickness.

1 To make the omelette, whisk the eggs, water, coriander and seasoning in a small bowl. Heat the oil in a wok. Pour in the eggs, then tilt the wok so that the mixture spreads in an even layer. Cook over a high heat until the edges are slightly crisp.

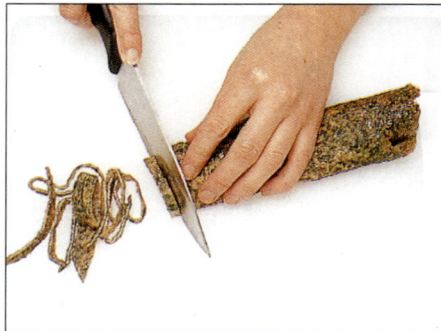

2 Flip the omelette over with a spatula and cook the other side for about 30 seconds until lightly browned. Turn the omelette on to a board and leave to cool. When cold, roll up loosely and cut into thin slices. Wipe the wok clean.

3 In a bowl, blend together the cornflour, sherry, chilli sauce and stock to make the glaze. Set aside.

4 Heat the wok until hot, add the oil and swirl it around. Add the ginger and spring onions and stir-fry for a few seconds to flavour the oil. Add the mangetouts, sliced pepper, mushrooms and water chestnuts and stir-fry for 3 minutes.

5 Add the beansprouts and Chinese cabbage and stir-fry for 2 minutes.

6 Pour in the glaze ingredients and cook, stirring for about 1 minute until the glaze thickens and coats the vegetables. Turn the vegetables on to a warmed serving plate and top with the omelette shreds. Serve at once.

Tofu Stir-fry

The tofu has a pleasant creamy texture, which contrasts delightfully with the crunchy stir-fried vegetables. Make sure you buy firm tofu which is easy to cut neatly.

INGREDIENTS

Serves 2–4

115g/4oz hard white cabbage
2 green chillies
225g/8oz firm tofu
45ml/3 tbsp vegetable oil
2 cloves garlic, crushed
3 spring onions, chopped
175g/6oz French beans, topped and tailed
175g/6oz baby sweetcorn, halved
115g/4oz beansprouts
45ml/3 tbsp smooth peanut butter
25ml/1½ tbsp dark soy sauce
300ml/½ pint/1¼ cups coconut milk

1 Shred the white cabbage. Carefully remove the seeds from the chillies and chop finely. Wear rubber gloves to protect your hands, if necessary.

2 Cut the tofu into strips.

3 Heat the wok, then add 30ml/ 2 tbsp of the oil. When the oil is hot, add the tofu, stir-fry for 3 minutes and remove. Set aside. Wipe out the wok with kitchen paper.

4 Add the remaining oil. When it is hot, add the garlic, spring onions and chillies and stir-fry for 1 minute. Add the French beans, sweetcorn and beansprouts and stir-fry for a further 2 minutes.

5 Add the peanut butter and soy sauce to the wok. Stir well to coat the vegetables. Add the tofu to the vegetables in the wok.

6 Pour the coconut milk over the vegetables, simmer for 3 minutes and serve immediately.

— COOK'S TIP —

There are literally hundreds of varieties of chilli. Generally speaking, dark green chillies are hotter than paler green ones, which are, in turn, hotter and less sweet than red chillies – but this is not a hard-and-fast rule and it is possible to be caught out by an unfamiliar variety. The "heat factor" of chillies is measured in Scoville units, with sweet peppers at 0 at the bottom of the scale and Mexican habanero chillies at 300,000, the hottest at the top. Most oriental recipes call for medium to hot chillies. Some Indonesian and Thai dishes can be very fiery, but Chinese recipes tend to use fairly mild fresh green or red chillies.

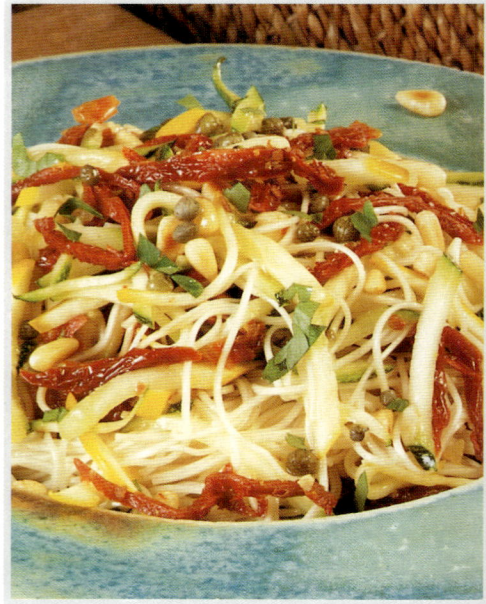

RICE &
NOODLE
DISHES

~

Oriental Fried Rice

This is a great way to use leftover cooked rice. Make sure the rice is very cold before attempting to fry it, as warm rice will become soggy. Some supermarkets sell frozen cooked rice.

INGREDIENTS

Serves 4–6
75ml/5 tbsp oil
115g/4oz shallots, halved and thinly sliced
3 garlic cloves, crushed
1 red chilli seeded and finely chopped
6 spring onions, finely chopped
1 red pepper, seeded and finely chopped
225g/8oz white cabbage, finely shredded
175g/6oz cucumber, finely chopped
50g/2oz frozen peas, thawed
3 eggs, beaten
5ml/1 tsp tomato purée
30ml/2 tbsp lime juice
1.5ml/¼ tsp Tabasco sauce
675g/1½lb cooked white rice, cooled
115g/4oz/1 cup cashew nuts, roughly chopped
30ml/2 tbsp chopped fresh coriander, plus extra to garnish
salt and ground black pepper

1 Heat the oil in a large preheated wok or non-stick frying pan and cook the shallots until very crisp and golden. Remove with a slotted spoon and drain on kitchen paper.

2 Add the garlic and chilli and cook for 1 minute. Add the spring onions and red pepper and cook for 3–4 minutes, or until the onions are beginning to soften.

COOK'S TIP

675g/1½lb cooked rice is equivalent to 225g/8oz raw weight.

3 Add the cabbage, cucumber and peas and cook for a further 2 minutes.

4 Make a gap in the ingredients in the wok or frying pan and add the beaten eggs. Scramble the eggs, stirring occasionally, and then stir them into the vegetables.

5 Add the tomato purée, lime juice and Tabasco sauce and stir well to combine.

6 Increase the heat and add the cooked rice, cashew nuts, coriander and plenty of seasoning. Stir-fry for 3–4 minutes, until piping hot. Serve garnished with the crisp shallots and extra fresh coriander, if liked.

Sushi

INGREDIENTS

Makes 8–10

For the tuna sushi

3 sheets nori (paper-thin seaweed)
150g/5oz fresh tuna fillet, cut
  into fingers
5ml/1 tsp wasabi (Japanese horseradish)
6 young carrots, blanched
450g/1lb/6 cups cooked Japanese rice

For the salmon sushi

2 eggs
2.5ml/½ tsp salt
10ml/2 tsp sugar
5 sheets nori
450g/1lb/6 cups cooked Japanese rice
150g/5oz fresh salmon fillet, cut
  into fingers
5ml/1 tsp wasabi paste
½ small cucumber, cut into strips

1 To make the tuna sushi, spread half a sheet of nori on to a bamboo mat, lay strips of tuna across the full length and season with the thinned wasabi. Place a line of blanched carrot next to the tuna and roll tightly. Moisten the edge with water and seal.

2 Place a square of damp wax paper on to the bamboo mat, then spread evenly with sushi rice. Place the non-wrapped tuna along the centre and wrap tightly, enclosing the nori completely. Remove the paper and cut into neat rounds with a wet knife.

3 To make the salmon sushi, make a simple flat omelette by beating together the eggs, salt and sugar. Heat a large non-stick pan, pour in the egg mixture, stir briefly and allow to set. Transfer to a clean dish towel and cool.

4 Place the nori on to a bamboo mat, cover with the omelette, and trim to size. Spread a layer of rice over the omelette, then lay strips of salmon across the width. Season the salmon with the thinned wasabi, then place a strip of cucumber next to the salmon. Fold the bamboo mat in half. Cut into neat rounds with a wet knife.

Indonesian Fried Rice

This fried rice dish makes an ideal supper on its own or as an accompaniment to another dish.

INGREDIENTS

Serves 4–6

4 shallots, roughly chopped
1 fresh red chilli, seeded and chopped
1 garlic clove, chopped
thin sliver of dried shrimp paste
45ml/3 tbsp vegetable oil
225g/8oz boneless lean pork, cut into fine strips
175g/6oz long grain white rice, boiled and cooled
3–4 spring onions, thinly sliced
115g/4oz cooked peeled prawns
30ml/2 tbsp sweet soy sauce (*kecap manis*)
chopped fresh coriander and fine cucumber shreds, to garnish

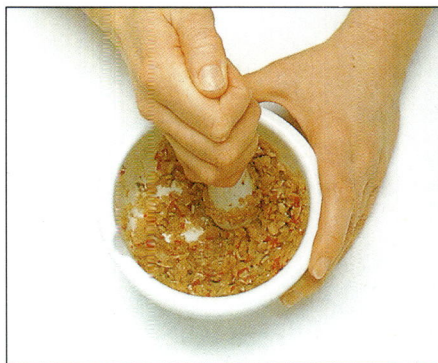

1 In a mortar pound the shallots, chilli, garlic and shrimp paste with a pestle until they form a paste.

COOK'S TIP

Shrimp paste, sometimes called dried shrimp paste, is a strong-smelling and flavoursome paste made from fermented shrimps that is used extensively in many oriental cuisines. Always use sparingly. It is available from most oriental food stores and Chinese supermarkets.

2 Heat a wok until hot, add 30ml/ 2 tbsp of the oil and swirl it around. Add the pork and stir-fry for 2–3 minutes. Remove the pork from the wok, set aside and keep warm.

3 Add the remaining oil to the wok. When hot, add the spiced shallot paste and stir-fry for about 30 seconds.

4 Reduce the heat. Add the rice, sliced spring onions and prawns. Stir-fry for 2–3 minutes. Add the pork and sprinkle over the soy sauce. Stir-fry for 1 minute. Serve at once, garnished with chopped fresh coriander and cucumber shreds.

Singapore Rice Vermicelli

Simple and speedily prepared, this lightly curried rice noodle dish is a full meal in a bowl.

INGREDIENTS

Serves 4

225g/8oz dried rice vermicelli
15ml/1 tbsp vegetable oil
1 egg, lightly beaten
2 garlic cloves, finely chopped
1 large fresh red or green chilli, seeded and finely chopped
15ml/1¼ tbsp medium curry powder
1 red pepper, seeded and thinly sliced
1 green pepper, seeded and sliced
1 carrot, cut into matchsticks
1.5ml/¼ tsp salt
60ml/4 tbsp vegetable stock
115g/4oz cooked peeled prawns, thawed if frozen
75g/3oz lean ham, diced
15ml/1 tbsp light soy sauce

1 Put the rice vermicelli into a heatproof bowl and cover with boiling water. Set aside to soak for 4 minutes, or according to the instructions on the packet, then drain thoroughly and set aside until required.

2 Heat 5ml/1 tsp of the oil in a preheated wok or frying pan. Add the egg and scramble until set. Remove with a slotted spoon and set aside.

3 Wipe out the wok and heat the remaining oil in the clean pan. Add the garlic and chilli and stir-fry for a few seconds, then stir in the curry powder. Cook for 1 minute, stirring, then stir in the peppers, carrot sticks, salt and stock.

4 Bring to the boil. Add the prawns, ham, scrambled egg, rice vermicelli and soy sauce. Mix thoroughly. Cook, stirring constantly, until all the liquid has been absorbed and the mixture is hot. Serve at once.

Toasted Noodles with Vegetables

Slightly crisp noodle cakes topped with vegetables make a superb dish.

INGREDIENTS

Serves 4

175g/6oz dried egg vermicelli
15ml/1 tbsp vegetable oil
2 garlic cloves, finely chopped
115g/4oz baby corn cobs
115g/4oz fresh shiitake mushrooms
3 celery sticks, sliced
1 carrot, sliced diagonally
115g/4oz mangetout
75g/3oz canned bamboo shoots,
    drained and sliced
15ml/1 tbsp cornflour
15ml/1 tbsp cold water
15ml/1 tbsp dark soy sauce
5ml/1 tsp caster sugar
300ml/½ pint/1¼ cups vegetable stock
salt and freshly ground white pepper
spring onion curls, to garnish

1 Bring a saucepan of water to the boil. Add the egg vermicelli and cook according to the instructions on the packet until just tender. Drain, refresh under cold water, drain again, then dry thoroughly on kitchen paper.

2 Heat 2.5ml/½ tsp oil in a preheated wok or frying pan. When it starts to smoke, spread half the noodles over the base. Fry for 2–3 minutes until lightly toasted. Carefully turn the noodles over (they stick together like a cake), fry the other side, then slide on to a heated serving plate. Repeat with the remaining noodles to make two cakes. Set aside and keep hot.

3 Heat the remaining oil in the clean pan, then fry the garlic for a few seconds. Halve the corn cobs and mushrooms and add to the pan. Stir-fry for 3 minutes, adding a little water, if needed, to prevent the mixture from burning. Add the celery, carrot, mangetout and bamboo shoots. Stir-fry for another 2 minutes, or until the vegetables are tender, but still firm to the bite.

4 Mix the cornflour with the water to form a smooth paste. Add the mixture to the pan, together with the soy sauce, sugar and vegetable stock. Cook, stirring constantly, until the sauce thickens. Season to taste with salt and white pepper. Divide the vegetable mixture between the noodle cakes, garnish with the spring onion curls and serve immediately. Each noodle cake serves two people.

Udon Pot

INGREDIENTS

Serves 4

350g/12oz dried udon noodles

1 large carrot, cut into bite-size chunks

225g/8oz chicken breasts or thighs, skinned and cut into bite-size pieces

8 raw king prawns, peeled and deveined

4–6 Chinese cabbage leaves, cut into short strips

8 shiitake mushrooms, stems removed

50g/2oz mange-touts, topped and tailed

1.5 litres/2½ pints/6¼ cups chicken stock or instant bonito stock

30ml/2 tbsp mirin

soy sauce, to taste

1 bunch spring onions, finely chopped, 30ml/2 tbsp grated fresh root ginger, lemon wedges, and extra soy sauce, to serve

1 Cook the noodles until just tender, following the directions on the packet. Drain, rinse under cold water and drain again. Blanch the carrot in boiling water for 1 minute, then drain.

2 Spoon the noodles and carrot chunks into a large saucepan or flameproof casserole, and arrange the chicken breasts or thighs, prawns, Chinese cabbage leaves, mushrooms and mange-touts on top.

3 Bring the stock to the boil in a saucepan. Add the mirin and enough soy sauce to taste. Pour the stock over the noodles. Cover the pan or casserole, bring to the boil over a moderate heat, then simmer gently for 5–6 minutes until all the ingredients are cooked.

4 Serve with chopped spring onions, grated ginger, lemon wedges and a little soy sauce.

Combination Chow Mein

INGREDIENTS

Serves 4–6

450g/1lb thick egg noodles

45ml/3 tbsp vegetable oil

2 garlic cloves, chopped

2 spring onions, cut into short lengths

50g/2oz pork fillet, sliced, or Chinese roast pork cut into short lengths

50g/2oz pig's liver, sliced

75g/3oz raw prawns, peeled and deveined

50g/2oz prepared squid, sliced

50g/2oz cockles or mussels

115g/4oz watercress, leaves stripped from the stems

2 red chillies, seeded and finely sliced

30–45ml/2–3 tbsp soy sauce

15ml/1 tbsp sesame oil

salt and freshly ground black pepper

1 Cook the egg noodles in a large saucepan of boiling water until just tender. Drain thoroughly.

2 Heat the oil in a wok and fry the garlic and spring onions for about 30 seconds. Add the pork fillet, if using, with the liver, prawns, squid and cockles or mussels. Stir-fry for 2 minutes over a high heat.

3 Add the watercress and chillies to the wok and stir-fry for a further 3–4 minutes, until the meat is cooked.

4 Add the drained noodles, stirring constantly but gently. Toss in the Chinese roast pork, if using, and add the soy sauce with salt and pepper to taste. Cook until the noodles are thoroughly heated through. Stir in the sesame oil, mix well and serve.

Tossed Noodles with Seafood

INGREDIENTS

Serves 4–6

350g/12oz thick egg noodles
60ml/4 tbsp vegetable oil
3 slices fresh root ginger, grated
2 garlic cloves, finely chopped
225g/8oz mussels or clams
225g/8oz raw prawns, peeled
225g/8oz squid, cut into rings
115g/4oz oriental fried fish cake, sliced
1 red pepper, seeded and cut into rings
50g/2oz sugar snap peas, topped
  and tailed
30ml/2 tbsp soy sauce
2.5ml/½ tsp sugar
120ml/4fl oz/½ cup stock or water
15ml/1 tbsp cornflour
5–10ml/1–2 tsp sesame oil
salt and freshly ground black pepper
2 spring onions, chopped, and 2 red
  chillies, seeded and chopped,
  to garnish

1 Cook the noodles in a large saucepan of boiling water until just tender. Drain, rinse under cold water and drain well.

2 Heat the oil in a wok or large frying pan. Fry the ginger and garlic for 30 seconds. Add the mussels or clams, prawns and squid and stir-fry for about 4–5 minutes until the seafood changes colour. Add the fish cake slices, red pepper rings and sugar snap peas and stir well.

3 In a bowl, mix the soy sauce, sugar, stock or water and cornflour. Stir into the seafood and bring to the boil. Add the noodles and cook until they are heated through.

4 Add the sesame oil to the wok or pan and season with salt and pepper to taste. Serve at once, garnished with the spring onions and red chillies.

Noodles with Spicy Meat Sauce

INGREDIENTS

Serves 4–6

30ml/2 tbsp vegetable oil
2 dried red chillies, chopped
5ml/1 tsp grated fresh root ginger
2 garlic cloves, finely chopped
15ml/1 tbsp chilli bean paste
450g/1lb minced pork or beef
450g/1lb broad flat egg noodles
15ml/1 tbsp sesame oil
2 spring onions, chopped, to garnish

For the sauce
1.25ml/¼ tsp salt
5ml/1 tsp sugar
15ml/1 tbsp soy sauce
5ml/1 tsp mushroom ketchup
15ml/1 tbsp cornflour
250ml/8fl oz/1 cup chicken stock
5ml/1 tsp shaohsing wine or
  dry sherry

1 Heat the vegetable oil in a large saucepan. Add the dried chillies, ginger and garlic. Fry until the garlic starts to colour, then gradually stir in the chilli bean paste.

2 Add the minced pork or beef, breaking it up with a spatula or wooden spoon. Cook over a high heat until the minced meat changes colour and any liquid has evaporated.

3 Mix all the sauce ingredients in a jug. Make a well in the centre of the pork mixture. Pour in the sauce mixture and stir together. Simmer for 10–15 minutes until tender.

4 Meanwhile, cook the noodles in a large saucepan of boiling water for 5–7 minutes until just tender. Drain well and toss with the sesame oil. Serve, topped with the meat sauce and garnished with the spring onions.

Somen Noodles with Courgettes

A colourful dish with lots of flavour. Pumpkin or patty pan squashes can be used as an alternative to courgettes.

INGREDIENTS

Serves 4
2 yellow courgettes
2 green courgettes
60ml/4 tbsp pine nuts
60ml/4 tbsp extra virgin olive oil
2 shallots, finely chopped
2 garlic cloves, finely chopped
30ml/2 tbsp capers, rinsed
4 sun-dried tomatoes in oil, drained
    and cut into strips
300g/11oz somen noodles
60ml/4 tbsp chopped mixed herbs
    (such as chives, thyme and tarragon)
grated rind of 1 lemon
50g/2oz Parmesan cheese, finely grated
salt and freshly ground black pepper

1 Slice the courgettes diagonally into rounds the same thickness as the noodles. Cut the courgette slices into matchsticks. Toast the pine nuts in an ungreased frying pan over a medium heat until golden in colour.

2 Heat half the oil in a large frying pan. Add the shallots and garlic and fry until fragrant. Push the shallot mixture to one side of the pan, add the remaining oil and, when hot, stir-fry the courgettes until soft.

3 Stir thoroughly to incorporate the shallot mixture and add the capers, sun-dried tomatoes and pine nuts. Remove the pan from the heat.

4 Cook the noodles in a large saucepan of boiling, salted water until just tender, following the directions on the packet. Drain well and toss into the courgette mixture, adding the herbs, lemon rind and Parmesan, with salt and pepper to taste. Serve at once.

Noodles Primavera

INGREDIENTS

Serves 4
225g/8oz dried rice noodles
115g/4oz broccoli florets
1 carrot, finely sliced
225g/8oz asparagus, cut into
    5cm/2in lengths
1 red or yellow pepper, seeded and cut
    into strips
50g/2oz baby corn cobs
50g/2oz sugar snap peas, topped
    and tailed
45ml/3 tbsp olive oil
15ml/1 tbsp chopped fresh ginger
2 garlic cloves, chopped
2 spring onions, finely chopped
450g/1lb tomatoes, chopped
1 bunch rocket leaves
soy sauce, to taste
salt and freshly ground black pepper

1 Soak the noodles in hot water for about 30 minutes until soft. Drain.

2 Blanch the broccoli florets, sliced carrot, asparagus, pepper strips, baby corn cobs and sugar snap peas separately in boiling, salted water. Drain them, rinse under cold water, then drain again and set aside.

3 Heat the olive oil in a frying pan. Add the ginger, garlic and onions. Stir-fry for 30 seconds, then add the tomatoes and stir-fry for 2–3 minutes.

4 Add the noodles and stir-fry for 3 minutes. Toss in the blanched vegetables and rocket leaves. Season with soy sauce, salt and pepper and cook until the vegetables are tender.

DESSERTS

〜

Exotic Fruit Salad

A variety of fruits can be used for this Vietnamese dessert, depending on what is available. Look out for mandarin oranges, star fruit, pawpaw and passion fruit.

INGREDIENTS

Serves 4–6
75g/3oz/scant ½ cup sugar
300ml/½ pint/1¼ cups water
30ml/2 tbsp stem ginger syrup
2 pieces star anise
2.5cm/1in cinnamon stick
1 clove
juice of ½ lemon
2 fresh mint sprigs
1 mango
2 bananas, sliced
8 fresh or canned lychees
225g/8oz strawberries, hulled and
  halved
2 pieces stem ginger, cut into sticks
1 medium pineapple

1 Put the sugar, water, ginger syrup, star anise, cinnamon, clove, lemon juice and mint into a saucepan. Bring to the boil and simmer for 3 minutes. Strain into a bowl and set aside to cool.

2 Remove the top and bottom from the mango and remove the outer skin. Stand the mango on one end and remove the flesh in two pieces either side of the flat stone. Slice evenly and add to the syrup. Add the bananas, lychees, strawberries and ginger.

3 Cut the pineapple in half down the centre. Loosen the flesh with a small serrated knife and remove to form two boat shapes. Cut the flesh into chunks and place in the syrup.

4 Spoon some of the fruit salad into the pineapple halves and serve on a large dish. There will be sufficient fruit salad to refill the pineapple halves.

Tapioca Pudding

This pudding, made from large pearl tapioca and coconut milk and served warm, is much lighter than the western-style version. You can adjust the sweetness to your taste. Serve with lychees or the smaller, similar-tasting logans – also known as 'dragon's eyes'.

INGREDIENTS

Serves 4
115g/4oz tapioca
475ml/16fl oz/2 cups water
175g/6oz granulated sugar
pinch of salt
250ml/8fl oz/1 cup coconut milk
250g/9oz prepared tropical fruits
finely shredded rind of 1 lime,
   to decorate

1 Soak the tapioca in warm water for 1 hour so the grains swell. Drain.

2 Put the water in a saucepan and bring to the boil. Stir in the sugar and salt.

3 Add the tapioca and coconut milk and simmer for 10 minutes or until the tapioca turns transparent.

4 Serve warm with some tropical fruits and decorate with lime zest strips and coconut shavings, if using.

Fried Bananas

These delicious treats are a favourite among children and adults alike. They are sold as snacks throughout the day and night at portable roadside stalls and market places. Other fruits such as pineapple and apple work just as well.

INGREDIENTS

Serves 4
115g/4oz plain flour
2.5ml/½ tsp bicarbonate of soda
pinch of salt
30ml/2 tbsp granulated sugar
1 egg
90ml/6 tbsp water
30ml/2 tbsp shredded coconut or
   15ml/1 tbsp sesame seeds
4 firm bananas
oil for frying
30ml/2 tbsp honey, to serve (optional)
sprigs of mint, to decorate

1 Sift the flour, bicarbonate of soda and salt into a bowl. Stir in the granulated sugar. Whisk in the egg and add enough water to make quite a thin batter.

2 Whisk in the shredded coconut or sesame seeds.

3 Peel the bananas. Carefully cut each one in half lengthways, then in half crossways.

4 Heat the oil in a wok or deep frying pan. Dip the bananas in the batter, then gently drop a few into the oil. Fry until golden brown.

5 Remove from the oil and drain on kitchen paper. Serve immediately with honey, if using, and decorate with sprigs of mint.

Mango and Coconut Stir-fry

Choose a ripe mango for this recipe. If you buy one that is a little under-ripe, leave it in a warm place for a day or two before using.

INGREDIENTS

Serves 4
¼ coconut
1 large, ripe mango
juice of 2 limes
rind of 2 limes, finely grated
15ml/1 tbsp sunflower oil
15g/½ oz butter
30ml/2 tbsp clear honey
crème fraîche, to serve

1 Prepare the coconut flakes by draining the milk from the coconut and peeling the flesh with a vegetable peeler.

2 Peel the mango. Cut the stone out of the middle of the fruit. Cut each half of the mango into slices.

3 Place the mango slices in a bowl and pour over the lime juice and rind, to marinate them.

4 Meanwhile heat a wok, then add 10ml/2 tsp of the oil. When the oil is hot, add the butter. When the butter has melted, stir in the coconut flakes and stir-fry for 1–2 minutes until the coconut is golden brown. Remove and drain on kitchen paper. Wipe out the wok. Strain the mango slices, reserving the juice.

5 Heat the wok and add the remaining oil. When the oil is hot, add the mango and stir-fry for 1–2 minutes, then add the juice and allow to bubble and reduce for 1 minute. Stir in the honey, sprinkle on the coconut flakes and serve with crème fraîche.

COOK'S TIP

You can sometimes buy "fresh" coconut that has already been cracked open and is sold in pieces ready for use from supermarkets, but buying the whole nut ensures greater freshness. Choose one that is heavy for its size and shake it so that you can hear the milk sloshing about. A "dry" coconut will almost certainly have rancid flesh. You can simply crack the shell with a hammer, preferably with the nut inside a plastic bag, but it may be better to pierce the two ends with a sharp nail or skewer first in order to collect and save the coconut milk. An alternative method is to drain the milk first and then heat the nut briefly in the oven until it cracks. Whichever method you choose, it is then fairly easy to extract the flesh and chop or shave it.

INDEX

aubergine: beef curry, 51

baked lobster with
black beans, 4 0
bamboo shoots and Chinese
    mushrooms, 70
bananas, fried, 92
basil: and chicken , 57
    and mussels, 41
beans: and lobster, 40
    and tofu, 72
beef: curry, 51, 52
    mange-outs, 50
    stir-fry, 48
    sukiyaki beef, 53
beetroot stir-fry, 64

chicken: chicken and buckwheat
    noodle soup, 18
    gingered, 58
satay chicken, 54
    stir-fried, 57
    sweet-and-sour, 56
    Szechuan, 59
chilli: potato and onion, 66
    prawns, 38
Chinese greens and fish, 30
Chinese sprouts, 65
Chinese-spiced fish, 27
chow mein, 84
coconut: mango stir-fry, 94
    meat patties, 24
    vegetables, 68
coriander: fish, 16
    omelette, 74
courgette noodles, 66, 88
crab and tofu dumplings, 21
crisp pork meatballs laced with
    noodles, 45
cucumber: fish cakes, 23
    stir-fried, 70

eggs 46, 70, 74

fish: Chinese-spiced, 27
    fish balls with Chinese greens,
    30
    fish cakes with
    cucumber relish, 23
    sliced fish and coriander soup,
    16
    spicy fish, 32
    sweet and sour, 34
    vinegar fish, 29
fragrant Thai meatballs, 46
fruit, exotic fruit salad, 91

ginger: chicken noodles, 58
    scallops, 38
green beef curry with Thai
    aubergine, 51
green curry of prawns, 37

Indonesian fried rice, 81
Indonesian potatoes with onions
    and chilli sauce, 66
Indonesian-style satay
    chicken, 54

lemon grass prawns on a crisp
    noodle base, 36
lemon-grass-and-basil-scented
    mussels, 41

lime: with pak choi, 73
lobster and beans, 40

mangetouts: stir-fried beef with
    mangetouts, 50
mango coconut stir-fry, 94
meat preparation, 13
miso breakfast soup, 19
mooli, beetroot and
    carrot stir-fry, 64
mushrooms: bamboo, 70
    pak choi, 62
mussels: lemon-grass-and-basil-
    scented mussels, 41

noodles: chicken and buckwheat
    noodle soup, 18
    courgettes, 66
    meatballs, 45
    ginger chicken, 58
    pork and noodle broth with
    prawns, 15
    prawns, 36
    Primavera, 88
    Somen noodles with

courgettes, 88
toasted noodles with
    vegetables, 83
tossed noodles with
    seafood, 86
udon pot, 84
    with spicy meat sauce, 86

onions: potatoes with onions and
    chilli sauce, 66

Oriental fried rice, 79

pak choi and mushroom
    stir-fry, 62
pak choi with lime, 73
parsnips: beef stir-fry with crisp
    parsnips, 48
peanuts: thick beef curry in sweet
    peanut sauce, 52
pork: and noodle broth with
    prawns, 15
    and vegetable stir-fry, 43
    meatballs, 45
    sweet and sour, 44
potato: Indonesian potatoes with
    onions and chilli, 66
prawns: chilli prawns, 38
    green curry, 37
    lemon grass and
    noodles, 36
    pork and noodle broth with
    prawns, 15
    quick-fried, 20
    sweet potato and pumpkin
    prawn cakes, 22

rice: Indonesian fried, 81
    Oriental fried, 79
    Singapore rice, 82

salmon, teriyaki, 28
scallops with ginger, 38
seafood: preparation, 13
    tossed noodles, 86
sliced fish and
    coriander soup, 16
Somen noodles
    with courgettes, 88
spiced vegetables
    with coconut, 68
spicy fish, 32
spicy meat patties
    with coconut, 24
spinach and tofu soup, 16
sprouts: Chinese, 65
squid: from Madura, 32
    stir-fried five-spice squid, 35
steaming, 6
stir-fried tomatoes, cucumber
    and eggs, 70
stir-frying, 6, 9
stuffed Thai omelette, 46
sukiyaki beef, 53
sushi, 80
sweet and sour fish, 34
sweet potato and pumpkin
    prawn cakes, 22
sweetcorn fritters, 24
Szechuan chicken, 59

tapioca pudding, 92
teriyaki salmon, 28
Thai sweet and sour pork, 44
thick beef curry in sweet peanut
    sauce, 52
toasted noodles with
    vegetables, 83
tofu: and crab, 21
    and green bean red curry, 72
    and spinach, 16
    stir-fry, 76
tomatoes with stir-fried cucumber
    and eggs, 70
tossed noodles with
    seafood, 86

udon pot, 84

vegetables: pork stir-fry, 43
    preparation, 10-12
    spiced vegetables
    with coconut, 68
    stir-fried mixed vegetables, 61
    with coriander omelette, 74
    noodles, 83
vinegar fish, 29

wok, 6, 8-9